The Third Act

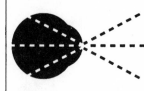 This Large Print Book carries the
Seal of Approval of N.A.V.H.

The Third Act

REINVENTING YOURSELF AFTER RETIREMENT

Edgar M. Bronfman

with Catherine Whitney

Thorndike Press • Waterville, Maine

Published in 2002 by arrangement with G. P. Putnam's Sons, a member of Penguin Putnam Inc.

Thorndike Press Large Print Senior Lifestyles Series.

The tree indicium is a trademark of Thorndike Press.

The text of this Large Print edition is unabridged.
Other aspects of the book may vary from the original edition.

Set in 16 pt. Plantin by Minnie B. Raven.

Printed in the United States on permanent paper.

Library of Congress Cataloging-in-Publication Data

Bronfman, Edgar M., 1929–
    The third act : reinventing yourself after retirement /
Edgar M. Bronfman with Catherine Whitney.
        p. cm.
    Originally published: New York : G. P. Putnam, 2002.
    ISBN 0-7862-4830-0 (lg. print : hc : alk. paper)
    1. Retirees — Psychology.   2. Retirees — Conduct of life.
    3. Retirement.   4. Self-actualization (Psychology)
    5. Large type books.   I. Whitney, Catherine.   II. Title.
    HQ1062 .B77 2002
    305.9′0696—dc21   2002073220

To Jimmy Carter —
my inspiration for the Third Act

Acknowledgments

My thanks to Griselda Warr, who did the interviews with me and was a big help. And special thanks to Catherine Whitney, for her fine work polishing the manuscript; and for the assistance of Paula Krafin, Lynn Wilson, and Hilary Ziff.

Contents

INTRODUCTION:

There *Is* a Third Act

There was never any doubt in my mind what my life's work would be. I started with Seagram the day I was born. I learned the business from the ground up, beginning as the lowliest clerk, learning every aspect as I worked my way up. My life as a businessman flowed through me. But unlike my father, the late Samuel Bronfman, I wasn't going to stay with Seagram until the day I died. I watched my father in his last years struggle to maintain an iron-fisted control of the company he had built. The company suffered, and so did he. He had prostate cancer the last two years of his life, and still he wouldn't let go. I couldn't really argue with him. The business was his life. It was his virility, and it was almost impossible for him to do other than what he did. But in the end he ruled by veto, not by imagination. Most of his decrees were based on the "not-invented-here" syndrome.

I was always determined that I would not be like my father in that respect, and so I retired as CEO of Seagram at age sixty-five and passed the baton to my son, Edgar Jr. I had asked him to join the firm sometime earlier, after he had tired of the motion picture business. He started as executive assistant to Phil Beekman, the COO. From there Phil recommended that Edgar Jr. go to London, and run Seagram Europe, where he did a superb job. Then I asked Edgar Jr. to return to the United States and take over the sales and marketing responsibilities here. By June of 1994, I knew he was ready to be CEO. I remained a nonexecutive chairman of the board, but I was able to let go of the day-to-day business. I realized that it no longer held the same fascination for me that it once had. My passion, and what had become my new life's work, was with the World Jewish Congress, the World Jewish Restitution Organization, and Hillel: The Foundation for Jewish Campus Life.

My relationship with my son, Edgar, is very different from the one I had with my father. We are very close, very affectionate. I have complete confidence in Edgar and his professional instincts. I know that for some CEOs, handing over the reins of the company is very traumatic. But for me it was infinitely easier — first, because I trusted Edgar, and second, because I had something meaningful to retire *to*.

Perhaps my father fought so hard to maintain control of his company because, for his generation, retirement meant the end of vitality and purpose. Life had only two acts: the years spent learning and the years spent working. Fortunately, my generation has been able to create a viable third act, and often it proves to be more gratifying than the first two.

The idea of writing a book about the wonderful opportunities of this Third Act came to me gradually. I firmly believed that a planned life after a business career was a necessity, but I hadn't heard much talk of it. So when I was given the opportunity to speak to a group of Stanford business students, I decided to present my idea about the Third Act to them. I didn't know what to expect. My audience comprised young people just starting out. Would they be interested in hearing about what they might experience thirty or forty years down the road?

To my amazement, the class was very attentive. They didn't slump back: They sat on the edges of their seats. I thought if young people who hadn't even started their careers could be so intrigued, surely there would be a tremendous amount of interest in the general public, especially those who were nearing retirement.

So, with the assistance of Griselda Warr, an amazing researcher, I proceeded to find interesting men and women in the Third Act of their lives, and interviewed them. They provided a wealth of insight, inspiration, and humor, and made writing this book a real pleasure. Later, Catherine Whitney helped refine the prose, and the result is a testimonial to a remarkable generation.

If there is one thing we found in common with almost everyone we interviewed, it's that they didn't plan the Third Act of their lives. As a result, they were often left feeling cut off and adrift, wondering what they would do with the rest of their lives. This was true even of those who had achieved much professional and material success.

Perhaps my young audience at Stanford,

where I first uttered the idea of planning for the Third Act, was just being polite when they showed so much interest in what I had to say. On the other hand, they may have sensed the truth of what I was saying — that as they embarked on their Second Act, it made good sense to keep the Third Act in mind. It's going to arrive at some point, and those who begin the process of planning ahead will be less likely to be shocked when the time comes.

It is my hope that this book will inspire many who have not yet considered the Third Act of their lives to start planning what they'll do and who they'll be in those years. It is not a how-to book, although the interviewees have plenty of good ideas. I think the tenacity and courage of many of them will be uplifting to those who cannot imagine making big changes in their lives after the age of sixty-five.

A friend of mine who is now in his mid-eighties told me that he would love to get his hands on the person who coined the phrase *the Golden Years.* He was the only survivor of a bomber that crash-landed during the Battle of Britain. His injuries were never completely healed. Yet he still hunts birds, still looks at the world with a sense of humor, and still chats up the girls.

I hope that for those who are approaching the Third Act of their lives, they can truly be Golden Years.

One

What Now?

The Shock of Retirement

Our primary purpose in our golden years is not just to stay alive as long as we can, but to savor every opportunity for pleasure, excitement, adventure, and fulfillment.

Jimmy Carter,
Former President of the United States

Former president Jimmy Carter is an excellent exemplar of the vitality and promise of the Third Act. He lives his life with pleasure and purpose and has made a remarkable contribution to the world since his forced retirement from politics some twenty years ago. But in spite of the quiet confidence that has characterized his public presence, he readily admits that the process of going from president of the United States to private citizen was very painful. After being defeated by Ronald Reagan in 1980, there were times he questioned himself and wondered if his active public life was over.

"Rosalynn and I were both distressed by our loss," he said recently, recalling the turmoil of that period. "Then, two weeks after losing the presidency, I found out from my blind trustee that for the first time in our lives we were deeply in debt. Our previously successful warehouse business had gone down the drain while we were in the White House, and we owed more than a million dollars. We had no plans for the future because we had really hoped and expected to be in the White House for four more years. Our last child was leaving the nest as Amy went off to school. So we came home. We hadn't lived in our house for ten years. Plains, Georgia, had a population then of just 600 and there were no job opportunities, especially for an ex-president of the United States. I had already made a public statement that I wasn't going to serve on corporate boards and go on the full-time lecture circuit and get rich. I didn't want to capitalize on my role as president to support us, and that left us kind of destitute.

"We needed a plan. So I signed a contract to write my presidential memoirs and sold my business for enough to pay off our debts. Next we decided to raise money for a presidential library — no easy matter for a defeated Democrat with no future public ambitions. But we were determined to establish a place where we could deal with world conflicts, a place where I could use my expertise as a mediator and my prestige as a former leader of the greatest nation on earth to bring people together to negotiate agreements and put an end to fighting. We had a mission. We had a plan."

The rest is history. Jimmy Carter has tackled the third phase of his life with as much passion and dedication as he had given to the first two. His life and the lives of countless others have been enriched by the vitality he has brought to the years since his forced retirement from the presidency. He is an inspiration to anyone approaching the last third of life who thinks they have nothing more to contribute.

ACTING OUR AGE

Was John Glenn acting his age when, at seventy-seven, he passed the physical exam to go back into space?

Horace Deets, Executive Director, American Association of Retired Persons

I hate the word *retirement*. I think the entire concept is obsolete, and old age has been transformed. The rules of aging have been forever altered as the lifestyles and life cycles of the older population have been reinvented. Old age has been reborn and renamed. A new stage of life — I call it the final third or the Third Act — has emerged full-blown. It's time to explore the vast potential of those years. Our ideas about old age are archaic, based on outdated models. We've got to update the data and draw new conclusions. Now when we talk about what it means to act our age, we're not talking about sitting in our rocking chairs, waiting for the sunset. We're talking about exploring new opportunities.

When the United States of America was incorporated in 1776, a child could expect to live to thirty-five years of age on the average. One hundred years later, life expectancy was still only about forty years. Because there was no significant older segment of the population, people weren't focused on the concerns of the elderly. If you were lucky enough to beat the odds and live till a ripe old age, you were put out to pasture to rock and reminisce.

When Social Security was introduced in 1935, barely 4 percent of the population survived to collect it. That's only 4 percent of the population surviving past the age of sixty-five. Times have changed.

The medical and socioeconomic breakthroughs of the twentieth century have created a brand-new statistical database. In the last century the life expectancy of the average American has increased by more than thirty years. Of all the men and women who have ever lived past sixty-five, more than two thirds are alive today.

In 1940 there were only about 3,500 centenarians in the United States, according to the official census records. Today there are over 60,000. In the year 2050 there will be over two million. The eighty-five-plus age group is the fastest-growing segment of the U.S. population. The baby boomers have become the "age boomers," soon to become members of the "triple-digit club."

Obviously the old model of retirement, i.e., backpedaling away from an active, productive role in society, is passé. We're living longer and are healthier than ever before. Most adults at sixty-five still have thirty or more active years remaining. In spite of overwhelming evidence supporting this, too many of us have not made the mental adaptation from thinking of "retirement" as the beginning of the end, to objectively viewing age sixty-five as the beginning of a rewarding new stage of life.

According to *Myths and Realities of Aging 2000*, a survey of the National Council on the Aging and the International Longevity Center, most Americans say they would be happy to live to be ninety, and almost half the survey respondents age sixty-five and older described their current stage as the best years of their lives.

Horace Deets, executive director of the American Association of Retired Persons (AARP), says that in light of such survey results, it's about time we change our outdated conventional wisdom about aging. "Was John Glenn acting his age when, at seventy-seven, he passed the physical exam to go back into space? Is Peter Drucker acting his age when, at ninety, he is still lecturing and writing books? The answer is yes, because there is no rule book for how to act at a certain age."

As the first generation to fully experience this stage, it is also exciting, uncharted territory. We can make the Third Act anything we want it to be.

IS THERE LIFE AFTER RETIREMENT?

"Should I have Post Toasties or cornflakes for breakfast?" is not a sufficiently important decision to keep you alert and interested in life.

C. Everett Koop,
Former Surgeon General of
the United States

Former surgeon general C. Everett Koop has an interesting take on the psychology of retirement. "If I had retired and put my feet up on the rail, I don't believe I'd be here today," he told me.

Anyone who knows Dr. Koop cannot imagine him putting his feet up. He's going to be going full speed until the day he dies. When I interviewed him, I wasn't surprised to hear that his passion for medicine began at a remarkably early age. "I started off in a single-minded pursuit of medicine from the age of five," he told me. "By age six I knew I wanted to be a surgeon. I haven't the slightest idea why, except that I knew that there were people who used their hands to cut people open and make them well, and that intrigued me. I used to sit and try to cut pictures out of papers with my left hand so I'd become ambidextrous. When I was in high school I used to get a little wooden matchbox and fasten a piece of black thread in it with a staple and then tie one-handed knots down inside the matchbox so that I would know how to work in small places."

Dr. Koop laughed when he recalled his precocious youth. "When I was a high school student I was already six feet tall. I weighed about 200 pounds and I looked a lot older than I was. On Saturday mornings I used to get on the subway from Brooklyn and go up to Columbia Presbyterian Medical Center. I walked in like I owned the place and headed upstairs, where I grabbed a white coat. Then I watched operations all day long. On Saturdays there was nobody else in the amphitheater, and surgeons are hams anyway — they love to talk to people. So they'd look up and see one eager face and they'd explain all the things they were doing.

"I was lucky in my career. I was in Philadelphia as an intern when Pearl Harbor came along. I was declared essential to the University of Pennsylvania for the duration of the war, so I had the opportunity to work at an extraordinary place, and I took a giant step forward. While I was still a resident I was appointed to be the surgeon-in-chief of the oldest children's hospital in America, and I assumed that role, although I did not yet have my boards. It takes two years to get those. And that was my first and only job until Reagan called me to be the surgeon general.

"I loved every minute of being surgeon general. I learned to shift my understanding from medicine one-on-one to public health. It came very naturally. I enjoyed policy making. I enjoyed being able to assess a situation and then work out a political way to bring it about, and I drew a real difference between a political compromise and a moral compromise.

"I used to wonder, is there life after being surgeon general? I didn't know really what I would do. I knew that I was excited by the ability to change things, not just for one patient, but for lots of people.

"My wife laughs about this episode, but the first job I was offered was to be the CEO of the American Cancer Society, and I said to her, worried, 'Betty, maybe I'd better take this. Maybe it's the only thing I'll be offered.' Well, within three weeks I'd had offers for everything from presidents of universities to chairmen of the boards of large companies, and I turned almost everything down, largely because I'm timid about money. However, I was able to pursue things that I wanted to one way or another, and I was on the faculty of four medical schools, and I love teaching. And then nine years ago I came here to set up the Koop Institute, which is devoted to reforming medical education in its broadest sense."

If C. Everett Koop has packed as much activity and innovation as possible into this Third Act, he is well aware that many of his fellow medical professionals are stopped dead in their tracks by the specter of retirement.

"I've seen the same destructive scenario played out over and over in my career, especially during my forty years in the department of surgery at the hospital of the University of Pennsylvania," he said. "I watch my colleagues turn sixty-five, and they're at the top of their game — sharp, innovative, creative, successful surgeons. Their patients do well, and everyone's happy. Suddenly everything changes, and the retirement guillotine drops. And then what happens to them? If you ask them 'What are you going to do with your retirement?' they say, 'Well, I want to travel.'

"I say, 'Okay. So you travel, and after about a year you've been every place you want to go; you don't want to get on an airplane ever again in your life. Then what are you going to do?'

" 'Well, I've always wanted to grow roses.'

" 'Okay,' I say, 'plant all the roses you want, spray all the beetles you want. Then what are you going to do? Roses don't grow all year.'

" 'Well, you know, I've got a wood lathe and I like to work on that wood lathe.'

" 'Okay, so you make candlesticks for every woman you know in the world; then what are you going to do?'

"They don't have any answers after that. But you know what happens to them? They cease to be interested in life and they follow their wives around in the supermarket and the only decisions they make are 'Should we get Post Toasties or cornflakes?' And that's not a sufficiently important decision to keep you alert mentally. I'm a firm believer in the facetious remark 'If you don't use it, you lose it.' "

MAKING A MENTAL ADJUSTMENT

My future is in my past, and my past is my present. I must now make the present my future.

Vladimir Horowitz

One day I had to be in Cambridge to give a luncheon talk to some Harvard business students. Griselda and I took advantage of being there to interview Mary Maples Dunn, head of the Schlesinger Library at Radcliffe, and a former president of Smith College. She had started her academic career on the faculty at Bryn Mawr and became dean before she moved to Northampton, Smith's base. She served as president of Smith for ten years. Now she had undertaken to help, for a one-year period, in the transition of Radcliffe becoming a full part of Harvard. Then she and her husband, a history professor at Penn, were planning to retire together.

"When I was ready to leave Smith, I surprised myself," she told us frankly. "I decided to go and see a psychotherapist to talk about what you do when your work life has ended. You see, I hadn't accepted this job yet, and I was thinking I was going to retire. I wanted advice: How do you organize your life after retirement? I found her quite helpful. She was very wise, although quite young, and helped me understand that when you leave a career, you do a little private grieving. After all, it's a loss in your life.

"What you have to do is concentrate on the things you'll do next. It became clear to me that volunteer work was really going to be a very important part of the next stage of my life. I belong to several not-for-profit boards that interest me a lot, and I'll probably devote myself to their programs. The organization that I now belong to which I find the most interesting is the NOW [National Organization for Women] Legal Defense and Education Fund. They just do wonderful work."

Bob Layton is a semiretired lawyer in New York City who runs the Senior Lawyers Committee of the New York State Bar

Association. He also talked about the psychological factors involved for retirees. He said, "My experience has been that if you don't resolve the mental adjustment, the ego problems, you cannot make the transition. Look at it this way. Most of us are primed for thirty-five years to be called 'Mr.,' to have secretaries and staffs who look up to us and do as we ask. Most of the lawyers I deal with can't even type a letter: They've had personal secretaries their whole lives. They don't know how to use a computer. They can't send a fax. Now, what an adjustment that is, to go into some little office somewhere where they have no secretary. They have to run a computer themselves. They have to make their own telephone calls. Their egos are not prepared for it. A lot of them can't do it.

"What I've found tremendously interesting," Bob went on, "is that the Bar Association's book the *Lawyer's Guide to Retirement* has nothing about psychological preparation for retirement — nothing! On every one of our programs we've had a psychologist. We consider it critical because lawyers — I can't speak for doctors or other professionals — but lawyers are atrocious at preparing for retirement. They can't face it. Denial is a big, big problem. I see many people who are hunting for ego-tripping titles or a way to make people think they're still important. In order to get them really engaged and willing to do some good, you've got to get them away from all the trappings of ego. Simply put, you have to get them willing to wear dungarees, come to work in a sport shirt, and just engage."

Bob introduced us to Ruth McCullough, a psychologist who specializes in helping people adjust to retirement. Her analysis lends valuable insight into the self-knowledge this transition requires. "People spend most of their time not being conscious of themselves," she said. "Consciousness means building an internal world as well as the external world. If you're not happy within yourself, if there isn't some kind of inner life, you're going to be adrift when your external reality changes, and that's very scary." She also remarked on the length of the life span that will take us into our nineties and beyond. "What will then be our purpose in life? To have any chance of happiness, one must respect that which one does with one's life, and must earn the respect of others.

"Retirement can be a real wake-up call," Ruth said, noting that the crisis is not about money but identity. Retirement — forced or not — is a new phase that's bound to be a shock to your system. "You suddenly have an enormous amount of time on your hands. What are you going to do with it? Your choice determines the quality of the rest of your life."

Ruth went on to say, "I think the word *retirement* should be thrown out. It is much more powerful and appropriate to think of yourself as moving to a new phase. If you're thinking about the next phase, there is a natural inclination to ask, 'How do I prepare for that? Who am I now? No title, no office, no purpose, no sense of belonging: Well, then, who am I? Is there a me, and who is that me? Am I just another golf player? Another granddad? How many charities can I be involved with? What's my purpose in life?' Consciousness means there's an internal world as well as the external world that we are building.

"I remember when my dad retired. He's seventy-eight now and he lives in England. He told me, 'I have too much time on my hands,' and I said, 'You are so talented. You have a beautiful voice. Why don't you go sing in a choir?' He said, 'That's a wonderful idea,' and now he sings in a choir and he travels around in Europe and he's having a great time. He didn't know what to do with himself. He also has a cottage in a very small village in the English countryside, and there are so many elderly people there that can't get around. I said, 'Dad, you're a fabulous driver. Offer to drive the elderly to their doctors' appointments. You will be the most popular man in your village.' It had never occurred to him. Being retired was almost like learning a foreign language."

Entertainment lawyer Bert Fields still works at his law practice in addition to penning successful fiction and nonfiction bestsellers in his "spare" time. He is currently working on a historical study of William Shakespeare. Bert shared his ideas about retirement. "Mandatory retirement is devastating," he acknowledged. "It can force you out of work in your prime. Be prepared. Plan for the next step before you've been forced out. I don't plan to ever officially retire from the law. My plan is to slow down the practice but keep my hand in, strategize, and consult. I'm going to keep on working in the field I love till I die, as well as trying some new things. You need to keep excitement in your life. You need activity. You need a plan. Give yourself a challenge."

John Carter Brown, director emeritus of the National Gallery of Art, and chairman of the United States Commission of Fine Arts, is perhaps the most eclectic of all the interviewees. He was sixty-five when interviewed in November of 1999. He told us, "I had fewer lives than most for the middle third. I worked for only one company from the day I left graduate school until the day I took early retirement. That was thirty-five years at the National Gallery of Art. I became director at age thirty-four."

I found it interesting that at the very beginning of his career Carter was already considering the implications of retirement. When he was at the Harvard Business School he was asked to choose a topic for a term paper, on the very broad subject of manufacturing. He chose the topic of what one would do with retirement. Even then, he felt it was a very significant topic. "I knew that we were going to have more leisure time," he said. "And so often businessmen throw so much of themselves into their careers that when their careers end, they go to pieces. They try golf for a few months and they get bored out of their minds and they don't know what to do. We did some statistical actuarial calculations, and retirement-to-death time spans for the 'type A' businessman was only 2.3 years. I felt that just in terms of living standards, Americans are going to be faced with what they do with their leisure and retirement time. They had better start planning for it now, rather than when suddenly they're out to pasture and it hits them that they have to find something to do.

"The hardest thing to lose when you retire," he continued, "are the perks. I remember when Ronald Reagan left the White House, it was reported that he had to dial the first telephone call in twenty years himself, carry his own briefcase, and so forth. You get used to the service and all the sycophancy. People laugh at your jokes and think that you're a lot better than maybe you are because they're looking for an angle."

Carter has approached his Third Act with the excitement that comes from starting fresh. He told me, "Shortly after I left the National Gallery, I was approached to be chairman if this new television network called Ovation. It was a lot of fun to be chairman of a company that would start up from scratch, be creative, and fill a real niche. The American public is much more interested in the arts than a lot of people give it credit for. With the expansion of channel capacity that was predicted with the digital revolution, it seemed that, just the way bookstores can have books on a whole lot of different subjects, so can television. So I signed on with the extraordinary Hal Morse, who had, against all the naysayers, started the Learning Channel and then the Discovery channel ten years later. Hal Morse really gave the lie to the idea that intelligent television is a contradiction in terms."

John Carter Brown is a great example of renewal after age sixty-five. He is involved in endeavors that create new opportunities in the arts, rather than hanging on to past accomplishments.

SEIZING OPPORTUNITIES

There are many things you can do after seventy. You can begin again . . . again. I hope that I'm always beginning again.

James Earl Jones

Vartan Gregorian has long been cited as a true visionary. It's no surprise that this Iranian-born academic, whose résumé includes the presidencies of The New York Public Library and Brown University, and currently the presidency of Carnegie Corporation, would bring those visionary qualities to the Third Act of his life. We sat down for lunch at my office, and Vartan eagerly shared his ideas with me.

"In America we confuse three things," he said. "The first is career and job. We make our careers and our jobs identical, and it isn't always so. There are many waiters and waitresses in New York who understand this: They'll tell you that their job is waiting tables, but that their career is acting. But most people don't comprehend this. You can have many careers and many jobs or one career and many jobs.

"The second is leisure. The whole classical notion of leisure has disappeared.

Today we consider leisure free time. As a matter of fact, only in America is the expression used, 'I have time to kill.' Leisure, in the Greek and traditional sense, was not time to kill. It was time to invest in yourself — be alone, contemplate. That has been an alien concept in America, because we are very action-oriented at the expense of leisure. But we need time to recharge our batteries.

"The third thing we confuse in America are the functions of success and failure as natural elements of life. We value success, which is wonderful, but we don't teach people how to cope with adversity and tragedy and failure — and these are all a part of the cycle of life."

Vartan's insights are crystal clear; he has a fascinating personal story, full of lessons that have shaped his perspective.

"I was born in Tabriz, Iran, and I left home when I was fourteen. I went to Lebanon, went to a French school, and then came to Stanford as a freshman. But one of my teachers in elementary school told me something I never forgot: 'When you grow up, always remember three lessons: If you see a donkey carrying gold, do not say it's a golden donkey. It's a donkey carrying gold. When you see a donkey carrying a diploma back and forth, don't say it's an educated donkey. It's only a donkey carrying a diploma. And then when you see a donkey in a holy city, even Jerusalem, don't say it's a holy donkey. It's only a donkey in a holy city.' The more I think about it, the more I see that this simple tale about the donkey sums up so much of the means and ends of life."

Vartan did not plan for the third stage of his life. He dismisses the thought. "Another thing I tell students," he said, "is that life is not just planning but also seizing opportunities and being curious. My two friends Brooke Astor and Kitty Carlisle are examples. They're both curious and alive. They're interested in things. It's not how old you are, it's how much interest and curiosity you have.

"When I was president at Brown, I created an endowed chair only for retirees. Just because you were retired, you didn't have to be inactive. You could come and teach at Brown University. I got Alfred Kazin from New York, age eighty-four, to teach in the English department. Riled up everybody! I got Lord Quentin from England — a number of others. I told everybody, 'You have to be retired to be eligible.' "

Although Vartan insists that he did not plan for retirement per se, he did follow a practice that made the approach of the third phase of his life easier. "What I have done, somewhat unconsciously, is to sum up my life every eight or nine years — what I know about myself, what I know about my directions, my limitations, my potential, my possibilities. This has turned out to be a good thing. When you take stock like that along the way, you don't have to panic that one third of your life is left, now what are you going to do with it? But rather, you get sustenance from previous accomplishments, or questions that you've never been able to resolve or answer."

Vartan left me with one final thought. The Spanish word for retirement, *jubilar,* means jubilation. "Jubilation," he said. "There's no retirement party, there is jubilation. Jubilee. So the trick is how to create your final third to be a period of jubilation rather than ossification and withdrawal."

Two

Find Your Passion:

What Are You Going to Do with the Rest of Your Life?

When I talk about what it's like to grow old, I use the analogy of a river. As the river runs it has cascades and narrows, but toward the end it's a vast wide flow, an estuary, and that's the best part. It's rushing, taking everything with it. It's happy, it's satisfied, and it's fat. And that's what I am. I'm fat, satisfied, and happy.

Philip Johnson, Architect

Philip Johnson, one of the most influential architects of the twentieth century, is also a pundit, a curator and historian, and a vibrant force for new ideas and change. Now striding through his tenth decade, he continues to produce, to create, and to inspire.

Philip agreed to meet at my office to discuss the Third Act of his life. He presented himself with the confident air of a man at the peak of his powers. He made it clear to me that he didn't believe in the concept of retirement. As a mere kid of ninety-two, he wasn't even close to beginning to wind down. He scoffed at the very idea. "The notion of my kicking the bucket before 100 or 102 is ridiculous," Philip told me. "There's nothing wrong with me. I never get sick, and I've never had such fun in my whole life. I don't believe in the concept of old age anymore."

Philip attributes his never-say-die attitude in large part to his very beneficial collaboration with his geriatrician, Dr. Howard Fillit. Both doctor and patient agree that Philip was close to death when they first met twelve years before. Philip was still recovering from major heart surgery. His recuperation was slow, and he was bedridden with malnutrition and pneumonia. His surgeons held out little hope for his recovery, but Dr. Fillit saw things differently. With the help and wise counsel of this outstanding geriatrician, Johnson not only recuperated from his surgery but rose from his sickbed a new man, imbued with an unquenchable lust for more life.

"It was Dr Fillit who persuaded me not to give in to old age," Philip said. "If I'm going to enjoy everything, I've got to enjoy being old, too, don't I? So I've got a little arthritis in my foot, or I can't hear perfectly, or my eyesight is dimming. So what? I've got my spirit and my brain. I'm brilliant. I'm better at life now than I was even ten years ago."

With a twinkle in his eye, Philip added that his main thrust was to have fun. "I don't accept jobs that aren't fun," he said. "You see, there are only three reasons to work — the three F's: Funds, fame, and fun. I only have one reason left — fun."

Philip Johnson's powerfully positive attitude is the benchmark of a vital Third Act. There's valuable therapeutic power in concentrating on the positive aspects of aging while downplaying the less appealing aspects. The majority of those I interviewed subscribe to a state of mind much like that of Groucho Marx: Attitude is everything. Groucho said, "Except for an occasional heart attack, I feel as young as I ever did."

A NEW WORK PHASE

One of the things that separates us two-legged ones from the four-legged ones is that we have souls. So we have more to feed than our tummies. Think of the language we use: My heart sings, " 'I dance for joy,' 'Beauty is in the eye of the beholder.' " I think we're just born with this need to have beauty and art in our lives.

Beverly Sills

Staying interested in your life and the lives of all around you is an essential building block of longevity. Good mental health, active involvement, and love of life are the core elements of the Third Act. The best advice boils down to this: Keep moving forward, one step after another, one day after another, one challenge after another.

The attitude of "Onward and upward" is a common thread in the lives of successful Third Acts. It is the difference between aging and getting old. Dr. Richard Besdine, director of the Center on Aging at the University of Connecticut, wrote, "Aging doesn't necessarily mean a life that is sick, senile, sexless, spent, or sessile [immobile]."

In fact, the opposite is true. Better than half of all Americans between the ages of seventy-five and eighty-five are free of chronic health problems. That means that more than half of the "elderly" experience no illness or injury that interferes with their daily activities or lessens their enjoyment of life. Too many valuable people and their wealth of experience are being wasted because the mainstream of our society no longer provides a productive place for them.

A lot of wonderful opportunities presented themselves to me as I investigated the Third Act. I got to meet and speak with some of the most fantastic spirits I've ever encountered. None was more fun or more vibrant than America's most famous coloratura, who I have the pleasure of addressing as Bubbles Silverman, although she's most recognized by her millions of adoring fans as Beverly Sills.

She warmed to the subject of the Third Act and shared her wit and wisdom with me one day as we chatted in her office. "When I walked out of my singing career," Beverly said, "I was at the very top of my profession and my capabilities. I wanted to leave with everyone saying, 'It's too soon,' rather than 'When is that woman ever going to stop?' When I stopped I was the highest-paid opera singer in the world.

"My voice had a long nonstop career. It deserved to be put to bed with quiet and dignity, not yanked out every once in a while to see if it could still do what it used to do. It can't.

"I don't miss performing. I would not like to get into the bullring and face the bull again . . . in any sense of the word.

"I've done so many things since the end of my singing career that people don't think of me as an ex–prima donna, making a grand entrance at the Metropolitan Opera. I'm at work in the arts and the world at large. I like to feel that I'm making some kind of difference, and I'm having a good time with it."

This confidence, she admitted, didn't come overnight. "There was a sort of lull in my life between the New York City Opera and my move to Lincoln Center. I thought I would step back, do some charitable work, and become 'a lady who lunches.' It was a very bad idea. I just gained a lot of weight from all those lunches; I was not at all happy. During that time in limbo I kept looking for something to come along and put me back in the thick of things. That's where I'm happiest.

That's where I want to be."

I asked Beverly about the work she has done since her retirement.

"Retirement?" she laughed. "Actually I'm always retiring. I retired from singing in 1979 when I was fifty, then I ran the New York City Opera for ten years until 1990, when I really thought I'd retired. Then I became chairwoman of Lincoln Center for five years before stepping down. I think I've got at least one more job in me before I really retire. The truth is, unemployment scares the living daylights out of me. I'm not at my happiest if I'm not thoroughly involved with some project or another. I'm a real 'Put me in, Coach' kind of a player."

I had first met the enchanting Kitty Carlisle some forty years earlier at Round Hill in Jamaica. My wife Ann and I had gone there with a group of friends for a week. One evening, Ann and I were a little late for dinner, and everyone was seated at a long table in the dining area by the beach. Kitty was sitting at one end, with her wonderful looks on display. I was especially admiring of her beautiful mouth, and I leaned over and lightly kissed those smiling lips. To my delight, she laughed and gave me a huge smile. Thankfully, her husband, Moss Hart, didn't seem overly incensed.

After that, we sort of lost track. When I found out she was still active, it blew my mind. I immediately made an appointment for Griselda and me to interview her. She received us in her bedroom, as she had a slight cold. She was cheerful as could be and seemed delighted to see me again.

Her career had been amazing. From having been a successful actress and television personality, she had become chairman of the New York State Council on the Arts. After that stint was over, she went back to work as a solo performer. She's a gutsy lady! But beneath her ladylike exterior and charming manner beats the heart of a lioness. She spoke openly about what she had experienced during her later years. When, at the age of eighty-six, she was asked to step down as chairwoman of the New York State Council on the Arts she experienced her own forced retirement crisis. "I mourned for a while like any decent CEO, and I was very unhappy," she told me. "Where was the thrill of each new day? Where was the excitement? And then, finally, one day I woke up and said, 'You're a damned fool, Kitty. You've got at least one more string in your bow. Use it.' And I got on with my life. I've gone back to my night job. I'm singing and performing again. I'm getting engagements.

"When I retired from the New York Arts Council, I agreed to create an American Musical Theatre program and to sing ten songs for it. Now, I hadn't sung in more than ten years. My vocal cords were like an out-of-tune violin: The strings had all gone loose. I tried and tried, but couldn't get anything going. I practiced every day. It was like trying to push a twenty-ton truck uphill with my nose. The thing that saved me was sheer ignorance: I never realized that I was supposed to be defeated. I tell other widows, women of a certain age, that they need to get up and keep going. Find a new thing and get on with it. That's life."

Ms. Hart has been an inspiration at every age. The writer Marie Brenner profiled her in her recent book, *Great Dames: What I Learned from Older Women*, calling her "a walking exclamation point." The description fits.

A THIRD ACT FOR THE SELF-EMPLOYED

Everything I've done has been play, in a sense, of doing what I am interested in and really want to do.

Jane Thompson,
Architect and City Planner

There are many people who don't ever have to retire — at least, not in a traditional sense. Artists, some lawyers, writers, architects, shop owners — anyone who is self-employed. In a sense these people are very lucky, although self-employment brings its own set of difficulties.

Jane Thompson, an architect and city planner, is self-employed.

She is the founder and head of the very successful Thompson Design Group in Boston. She began this business on her own in 1993, at age sixty-six, when her husband and business partner, Ben, suffered a severe stroke. The stroke left him debilitated and unable to work. When we talked about the Third Act of her life, I wanted to know where Jane found the strength to go on after her life partner got sick.

"Well," she said, "I'm doing what I've always done, only now I'm doing it by myself. Ben and I worked together for thirty years at a large firm, but after his stroke I needed a change of direction. I decided to step forward and stand alone.

"It's not that I ever intended to retire. As a matter of fact, in the world of self-employment — or self-unemployment, as the case might be — there is no such thing. Retirement is a pretty ethereal concept when you're involved in the arts in any way. There's no way you could really say, 'I think I'm going to stop working.' The concept of retirement is simply not part of my consciousness."

Now that she must tend to Ben, she'll shape work in such a way that she can still run the company, guide the work, and deal with the clients. "There are young, energetic people who need to know what I know — people who have not been where I've been," Jane said. "So there's a continuing usefulness and I can give more time to projects in the city that need some good thinking that they won't pay for, like the whole new seaport development in South Boston.

"It's not like I've worked for a living and now I'm going to play," she went on to say.

"The problems that I really want to solve or think are worth working on solving — that's a fairly seamless thing. Now, when it gets to hobbling around and I'm unable to do it, I will find some area of usefulness within this total framework.

"Luckily," Jane added, "I've never had to deal with clinical infirmities or aging problems until I had some problems recently with my leg, which slowed down my walking. I tell all the young people in my office, 'My mouth and my brain still work, but my feet are a little slower for the moment. We'll all have to deal with it.' I believe in the power of *chi,* what the Chinese refer to as the life force. It's built in, the will to live, to persist, to endure, no matter how difficult things are or may seem to be. Live on, against the tide or with the tide, but live."

While it's true that artists don't experience the separation anxiety that comes with conventional retirement, they live lonely lives, and must be prepared for that. My wife, Jan Aronson, an artist, leaves the house early every day. Mondays, Wednesdays, and Fridays she swims at around 5:30 a.m. Then she breakfasts and heads for her studio in Long Island. She generally comes home after 6:30. On Tuesdays and Thursdays she is at the gym, bicycling for an hour and then lifting weights for another hour. Then she goes to the studio. She works hard, as most artists do, and she spends most days not seeing people as she brown-bags her lunch.

My sister, Phyllis, is an architect; she built the Canadian Centre for Architecture in Montreal. She decided at some point in her career to retire as chief executive of her company, but she certainly hasn't slowed down.

There are tradeoffs to every choice — whether it's working for yourself or others.

TAKING CHANCES

There is a transition when you leave a field where you feel you know more than anyone else about it. Then suddenly you're in a business where you have to listen to other people. We've been here fifteen years, and to this day I don't know when it's time to cut hay.

Miles Cahn, Age Eighty,
Coach Leather Founder
Turned Cheese Maker

Learning new skills and making bold changes in the Third Act is not only an exciting opportunity to expand your horizons, but an infusion of zest that capitalizes on a mature person's experience and mastery. Most Americans become skilled at several new — and often unrelated — jobs in a working lifetime.

The working lifetime no longer ends at sixty-five. Many successful older citizens are starting brand new ventures in the Third Act. Take the case of Miles and Lillian Cahn.

Miles and Lillian founded Coach Leather, one of the world's finest lines of leather goods. After devoting thirty-nine years to creating a highly successful company, they found themselves in their mid-sixties gearing up for a new venture — as goat farmers and cheese makers!

"It's not that we always wanted to raise goats, but we found this beautiful farm in Columbia County, New York, that was going out of business," Lillian explained. "We wanted to protect it and make it a viable farm once again. After considering the options, we decided to take it over, raise goats, and make and sell goat cheeses like those we had enjoyed so often in France. We jumped in, thinking Coach

Farm would be a weekend getaway and a weekend business venture. We were still running the leather factory, and for eighteen months we commuted back and forth from the factory to the farm, changing hats on the run. It was impossibly hectic. We were trying to build and create the farm business while continuing to run Coach Leather and the factory. We finally decided to sell one or the other. So we sold Coach Leather and now devote ourselves full-time to Coach Farm. The goats won."

At an age when the societal model tells workers to kick back and devote themselves to leisure activities, Miles and Lillian became farmers and cheese producers, a completely new career for them both. Miles laughed when I commented on what I saw as their courage in hewing out a whole new life for themselves. "I'm not sure that was the driving force," he said. "I think it was more the potential fear of failure and humiliation, of how silly we would look as failed goat farmers."

Miles decided to create a high-end classic French cheese and employed a gifted French cheese maker to help them create their signature products in a classic style. More than a decade later, it is apparent that they have been successful.

Steven Jenkins, noted *maître-fromager* and connoisseur, has praised Coach Farm cheese, and today the Cahns are farming over seven hundred acres. They have created another impressive success. It wasn't easy. Nothing good ever is.

"We're very pleased, but we didn't get here without a lot of hard work and a lot of stress," Lillian said. "During the first few years it looked like the whole project was impossible. We left a business where we were the experts and started a new venture as neophytes. We had to learn everything from scratch and rely on the expertise of others. We've been farming for fifteen years now, and we're still learning new things about the business. Not only have our lives taken a major turn, but we've been able to make a success of it."

NEW IDENTITIES

The great thing is I can go on writing and I can go on thinking all my life. Some people aren't as lucky when they're cut loose from their life's work.

Walter Cronkite

60

There used to be a parlor game in New York in which the participants would write down the name of somebody they would nominate to be the president of the United States had they that power. Then they would discuss the various nominees. Walter Cronkite's name came out on top quite often. I don't know whether it was the grandfatherly look, à la Ike, or that compelling voice, or the fact that he had so much credibility.

Walter Cronkite, while retired from being the *CBS Evening News* anchor, seems to have plenty to do with documentaries and other projects. He maintains his offices at CBS, which is where we interviewed him. He was a touch late fighting crosstown traffic, and as he drew near we heard that famous and still-familiar voice of his — so unmistakable.

This was the first time I had met him, and he was as fascinating as I had expected him to be. He said, "The emotional stress — I felt very much at sea when I was no longer in the newsroom every day. But I realized how much I missed it. That clicking teleprinter and the typewriters — which you can't hear anymore, the way they work now. But that sound was all part of the newsroom and it was the heartbeat of the news organization. I missed it a lot. I missed not being there when the news was breaking and doing something about it. Deciding who covered it, how it would be covered, getting on the story myself, that kind of thing. Getting on the telephone — I missed that a great deal. I still miss it, twenty years later. The other work is interesting and I think it's fruitful, but I miss that daily journalism."

I asked why he had decided to retire. He said, "I selected sixty-five as the time I was going to step down from the pressures of daily journalism. I had no intention of leaving journalism entirely, or even my association with CBS entirely, but my whole life had been involved with daily journalism. Eleven years with United Press, years with Scripps Howard before that, and then in television later. We were always fighting deadlines, and that's an exciting and wonderfully rewarding business as far as I'm concerned. No question about it being stressful. I didn't feel the stress so much as I desired to have more free time for myself and my family. I wanted to play a little more tennis and do a little more boating. I wanted be available for my family vacations when the children were out of school and that kind of thing. So I enforced my sixty-five-year-old intentions and stepped down from the *Evening News* at that time.

"I have not wanted for anything to do in the years since then at all. I write, lecture, appear in public forums, and make television, film, and documentary appearances on a regular basis. I have no 'terminal facilities,' as my father used to say. I still have a hard time rejecting an interesting project. Between my family and my work, my life is very full."

He ended our interview with a story, told with his signature wry good humor. "Recently I was in Yellowstone National Park, working on a documentary, when a lady approached me with a quizzical expression on her face. She tapped me on the arm and asked, 'Did anyone ever tell you that you look just like Walter Cronkite? I mean, before he died?' She paused for a moment and added, 'Except I think he was thinner.' With that I walked away completely, but my wife Betsy was still standing there. The woman turned to Betsy and she said, 'Walter Cronkite is dead, isn't he?' and Betsy said, 'Yes, I think he died of thinness.' "

Walter Cronkite's former CBS colleague, Mike Wallace, was eighty-one when we interviewed him. It was remarkable that he seemed just as thrilled to be at *60 Minutes*, and just as excited about the new story he was pursuing as he always had been. "This is the only thing that I've really wanted to do," he told me. Wallace is a self-proclaimed late starter. "I didn't really begin what I thought was a proper career in television news until I was thirty-eight," he said. "It took me a little time to find out what I wanted to do. I graduated from the University of Michigan in 1939 and I was convinced at that time I wanted to be a radio announcer. That's all I thought about. I walked into the campus radio station and I was convinced: That was it. And I got myself a job, first in Grand Rapids and then in Detroit, and then in Chicago, and I was making a fair amount of money and enjoying it. Then I went into the Navy and in the Navy I began to think, 'Just reading other people's words, whether it's commercials or doing an occasional interview [this is all radio], this is a bore, really, there's got to be more to it than this.' And that's when I decided, 'Hey, let's find my way.' It took me a little time to do that. I decided to single in on news. But there wasn't a lot of money to be made in news.

I mean, face it, you could make a lot more money doing commercials or narrating *The Green Hornet.*"

"When I came back from the Navy in 1946, though, it was the beginning of television. I wasn't sure that I was going to make it in television. Little by little I found my way. And I really had to start, in effect, from scratch because I'd not been a reporter since high school . . . I really found myself in the news business about the time I got to my middle forties. Then I realized that was my bliss. It wasn't a question of work. I went to work every day and it wasn't work." Wallace still claims it's not work. He can't imagine a better job. "Hell, I'm older than everybody here. Don [Hewitt] is the only one who even comes close: He's seventy-eight. But television is a collaborative undertaking, and the young people on my staff are my eyes and ears — and, to a certain degree, my brain."

How do you know when to stay and when to leave? It's not always clear-cut, and a great deal has to do with your profession. My good friend Dr. Neal Kassell, now in his late fifties, is a professor and vice chairman of neurological surgery at the University of Virginia Health Science

Center. Jan and I were down there for a visit and we started talking about the subject of retirement. Neal was telling me some problems he was having with his department, and I offered some advice, which he later thanked me for, saying it changed his whole perspective of retirement. The advice was simple: First, retire when you're on the way up, not when you've plateaued, and certainly not when you're on the way down. And the second was my often-stated contention that you should plan your retirement so that you retire *to* something, not *from* something.

Based on our discussion, Neal told me he had made some decisions about his own retirement. "The job that I do is very demanding," he said. "In academic surgery or academic medicine, you really have three parts to your job. There's patient care: seeing patients and operating on them. There's research and there's teaching, and then of course there's administration. It's a difficult balancing act, and at certain stages of your life you're better off doing one thing than another. For instance, you could argue that the ability to stand for hours in the operating room is easier to do when you're younger than when you're older.

"In academic medicine there's no mandatory retirement age, so in theory you could continue to do brain surgery until you're eighty or ninety, or until somebody deems you incompetent. It's very difficult for a surgeon to give up surgery, because surgeons in general, and especially the men, are very ego-driven, macho-type people, and for them to voluntarily say 'I'm going to quit' is like saying 'I don't have any more testosterone.' I've decided to announce, at this time, while there are years ahead of me, that I will give up surgery at the age of sixty-five to make room for younger people.

"The second piece of it is, what do I plan to do? Well, until I retire I plan to emphasize the clinical practice, whereas in the past I've done a lot of research. Then I'll pick up the research again at the time of my retirement. I've been casting about for how do you do research that's meaningful without killing things. You could use tissue culture or you could do things like that. But there's this whole area of information technology: How do you use that to better display things, to analyze things, to do interoperative navigation? That's an area I'm interested in.

"The second thing is that I'd like to get

back to teaching. Maybe college students or even younger. I miss teaching."

When I suggested to Neal that it sounded like he planned to be a real Renaissance man, he told me quite seriously, "I view medicine and surgery as a privilege, and a responsibility to the system that has invested a tremendous amount in getting me to the level where I am. I feel an obligation to pay back that system by staying in as long as possible. I also believe that medicine is a different calling than any other. There's no comparison. There is no experience you can imagine that is as satisfying and gratifying as saving another person's life. You don't give that up easily."

SEARCHING FOR NEW DIRECTIONS

Every person born in this world represents something new, something that never existed before, something original and unique. Everyone's foremost task is the actualization of their unique, unprecedented, and never-recurring possibilities.

Martin Buber

This quote by the great twentieth-century philosopher and activist Martin Buber is a touchstone of New Directions, an organization founded in 1986 that helps senior executives, professionals, and veteran athletes find and create full-and part-time jobs, business ventures, board directorships, consulting projects, philanthropic opportunities, and retirement pursuits. Steve Fitzgerald, an adviser to New Directions, and also a retiree (albeit an early one: He retired from IBM in his mid-fifties), is a man with a plan for change in retirees' lives. He told me that he sees too many clients who never gave a thought to retirement until it happened. It's the most common mistake he encounters. "We see a lot of retirees who thought they wanted to play golf seven days a week, and spend all their free time with their wives and kids. Then they discover that they don't like to play that much golf, and their wives don't like that much time with their husbands, and the kids don't want to see them at all. It's soon time to rethink retirement."

Steve observed that many successful people never think about how to spend the final third of their lives until they're in it, and they're bored by inactivity. "One thing I know," he says, "is you've got to have balance. Work. Play. Give back. Only with balance can you continue to grow. There are so many people out there who have a lot to give back but haven't figured out what or how to do it. Life expectancy has risen dramatically. It becomes more and more important to like, to care about, what you're doing in the last third of your life."

Nearly 35 percent of retirees hold some kind of job, some for financial need, many for emotional needs: self-esteem, self-worth, and companionship. Steve pointed out, "A lot of people are going to be doing some kind of work until they're eighty. It's so important to get involved in something that you really care about. What do you really want to do? What have you done? If you spent your life as a banker, is banking the extent of your knowledge? What other interests do you have? You have to carefully assess your interests and your skills before jumping into a new situation."

Steve is a busy guy. "I'm able to fit a lot into my day," he admitted with a laugh. "Work, consulting, volunteering, pet projects, future plans, and more. When I got home last night at 9:30, my wife laughed at me and asked, '*This* is retirement?' "

Three

Do Good:

A Time for Giving Back

There are three stages of life. The first is learning, the second stage is earning, and the third stage is giving back.

Hobart Gardiner, Director, International Executive Service Corps

The September 11, 2001, terrorist attack occurred just as I was completing work on this book. It was a devastating blow, one that wounded our hearts and troubled our souls. The horror was overwhelming, but I must say that the collective national spirit of giving that emerged from this great tragedy inspired me. Our flagging sense of community disappeared in an instant. In its place rose a groundswell of giving and sharing. Everyone wanted to make a contribution, to be part of the healing and restoration. It was an unprecedented time of national selflessness, a soaring example of the spirit that makes this country great.

Imagine what could be possible if that unstoppable desire to give back were constantly present in our lives. Consider the contribution that older Americans could make.

The United States today possesses the fastest-growing, best-educated, and most vigorous population of older adults in the history of the world. The senior population today is more than twice what it was in 1960, and it will double again in the next twenty years. By 2050, adults over sixty-five will outnumber the rest of the population in this country.

The wisdom, experience, talents, and skills of older Americans are going to revamp the face of volunteerism. As the first wave of the 75-million-member baby boom prepares to retire, the whole structure of volunteerism is about to be reinvented. There exists a virtual tidal wave of skilled professionals, talented individuals, and top-drawer executives who are ready to do good. An army of vigorous retirees is looking for important, creative roles as volunteers and consultants for nonprofit organizations.

Almost every person whom I interviewed for this book participated in volunteerism. In addition to their altruistic reasons — and these were substantial — my interviewees formed an enthusiastic chorus in favor of volunteering. The same comments were repeated over and over: Volunteering expands horizons, bolsters personal growth, provides enormous self-satisfaction, increases your circle of acquaintances and support, and is just plain good fun.

From my own experience working with the World Jewish Congress, Hillel, and other Jewish organizations, I can tell you it's a gratifying way to sum up a life's work. For many of us, our greatest legacy will come from what we do in the final third of our life. My personal hope is that I be remembered as a man who made a difference in this troubled world. Let's face it: We all want to make a difference.

According to the AARP, a full 38 percent of Americans over sixty-five have expressed a willingness to volunteer but don't know where to turn. We desperately need a national center for senior service, a clearinghouse for volunteerism. Unfortunately, it doesn't exist.

Volunteerism allows retirees to maintain or create a positive social role to replace roles lost in retirement. It gives meaning to life as well as provides structure, purpose, and a sense of community and personal growth.

BUILD A LASTING LEGACY

Living your beliefs is a rare virtue and greatly to be admired.

Katharine Graham

For me, giving back has meant doing what I can to inspire a renaissance of Jewish life. I admit, however, that my life as a Jew has been a metamorphosis.

I began my life with a weak sense of my Jewish identity, but my path has changed, and my sense of identity has been intensified. I wrote about that path in a memoir, *The Making of a Jew.* That's a story for another day, but the essence of the story has been the catalyst for my postretirement life, which is dedicated to my wish for a Jewish renaissance. I think it is a worthy pursuit. I'm trying in every way I can to teach young Jews the stories of their ancestors, the ethics of Judaism, and pride in their history. My goal is to slow the rate of assimilation through support of institutions such as Hillel, Jewish summer camps, day schools, and Jewish Community Centers. This is the hands-on work of my life since my retirement, and I believe it will be my most valuable legacy. When I herald the value of volunteerism, I speak from my heart. I want others to experience the tremendous gratification that has become a part of my everyday life. As my friend Kay Graham told me, "Living your beliefs is a rare virtue and greatly to be admired."

Two of the greatest advocates of volunteerism and senior service are Jimmy and Rosalynn Carter, especially in their highly visible association with Habitat for Humanity International. When the Carters left the White House, they were eager for meaningful work to further their lifelong commitment to community, social justice, and humanitarianism. They began by establishing the nonprofit Carter Center in Atlanta to promote peace and human rights. Carter Center fellows, associates, and staff join with President Carter in efforts to resolve conflicts, promote democracy, protect human rights, and prevent disease throughout the world. Over the years President Carter has monitored many elections in evolving democracies.

In 1984 the Carters also began their long association with Habitat for Humanity when they led a work group to New York City to help renovate a six-story building with nineteen families in need of decent, affordable housing. With that first project the seeds were sown for the annual Jimmy Carter Work Project, an internationally recognized event in the Habitat calendar ever since.

Each year Jimmy and Rosalynn give a week of their time as well as their considerable carpentry efforts to the Project. (It is a little-known fact that President Carter is a skilled carpenter, and Rosalynn is fast catching up: After years of practice with Habitat she wields a hammer with the best of them.) Volunteers from around the world join them at a different location every year to build homes and raise awareness of the need for affordable housing for all.

"We have become small players in an exciting global effort to alleviate the curse of homelessness," Carter said. "With our many new friends we have worked to raise funds, to publicize the good work of Habitat, to recruit other volunteers, to visit overseas projects and even build a few houses."

Jimmy Carter is at all times a modest man. In 2000 the Jimmy Carter Work Project built 157 houses in New York City; Jacksonville, Florida; and the Carters' home of Sumter County, Georgia. Other recent Jimmy Carter Work Projects have taken place in the Philippines (293 houses in 1999), Houston, Texas (100 houses in 1998), and Kentucky and Tennessee in 1997.

"Habitat has opened up unprecedented opportunities for me to cross the chasm that separates those of us who are free, safe, financially secure, well fed and housed, and influential enough to shape our own destiny from our neighbors who enjoy few, if any, advantages of life," Carter said.

Obviously, Jimmy and Rosalynn Carter are emotionally invested in the work they do for Habitat for Humanity. It's also clear that their association is a good fit. Habitat espouses many of the causes that have interested the Carters throughout their public life.

Finding the right volunteering project after retirement is crucial. Today's retirees are eager to contribute to important and diverse projects and tasks in a variety of worthy arenas, but many powerful executives and CEOs are completely ill-prepared to create exciting post-job jobs. Their lack of preparation for an engaging Third Act stops them cold, leaving them idle and frustrated. Too late does it become clear to them that getting to retirement was 95 percent of the fun — or, as the old Spanish proverb goes, "Sometimes the road is better than the Inn."

At age seventy-eight Eastman Kodak founder George Eastman shot himself. He left a sad note that read, "My work is done. Why wait?" What a waste of genius. Again I think of the words of one of my personal heroes, Jimmy Carter, who wrote, "It's a sign of maturity when we can accept honestly and courageously that frustrated dreams, illness, disability and eventual death are all normal facets of a person's existence — and that despite these, we can still continue to learn, grow and adopt challenging goals. You're only old when regrets take the place of dreams."

At life's crossroads we are all called upon to set a new path and adopt a new sense of purpose. Retirement is one of those crossroads, and for many retirees it has been decades since they were called upon to invent themselves and create a sense of self-worth. Finding a challenging and exciting way to give back can be the "tent pole" of a brilliant and gratifying Third Act.

A PLACE TO START

Personally, I want to die in an airport, briefcase in hand, mission accomplished.

Maggie Kuhn, Founder, Gray Panthers

There isn't a magic formula, as everyone has their own individuality and their own needs, wishes, and circumstances. There are, however, many sizes that might fit quite a few.

America has made management into a fine art. Good managers are still hard to find, probably because the most talented want to be on their own — and that's what makes our economy so robust. In many other first world countries the freedom of managers to act as they see fit is something to envy. Years ago Seagram had an office in Rome, which was overstaffed, under-worked, and overpaid. The problem was so pervasive, the only way to solve it was to move to Milan; we were quite sure that the staff would not move along with the company. In America that wouldn't have worked, but then in America such machinations aren't necessary. Here we find normal ways to run a tight ship. Many other less fortunate economies can use our managerial skills, and it should be an honor to help the less advanced economies to climb the ladder.

Hobart Gardiner is the president and chief executive officer of the International Executive Service Corps, a volunteer organization that pairs professionals with businesses, nonprofit organizations, and governments in 120 developing countries. Founded by Frank Pace many years ago under the auspices of David Rockefeller, the idea was, and still is, to use the expertise of retired managers to help foreign companies that need some managerial expertise to get on their feet. The organization puts business savvy to work in places where it is most needed. Gardiner has seen the difficulties facing retirees over and over again at the IESC.

"When people retire, they wind up feeling very frustrated because they feel that they are no longer needed," Hobart told me. "People stop calling. It's 'Who's

Who' to 'Who's He?' overnight. This is where we come in. We offer ways for these people to do something constructive, to remain active, to maintain a sense of dignity, and to do something really interesting. It's an adventure when you go out on an IESC assignment."

IESC has about 13,500 volunteers registered in the Skills Bank, with two to three hundred out on assignment around the world at any given time. The organization sends out about a thousand volunteers per year. Most are retirees; the average age is about sixty-eight. They cover a wide range of socioeconomic backgrounds and areas of expertise. What they all have in common is a desire to do something for others — to give something back.

"Our people tell me they get enormous satisfaction from helping, and they are moved by the friendships they find," Hobart said. "They also come home with bragging rights, a great story to tell their friends. There are lots of reasons why people volunteer, but finally it comes down to feeling good about yourself because you're paying back and doing something for your country."

Giving back is the primary reason for volunteering your time and talent, but it's not the only reason. Researchers consistently find that most older volunteers, when compared to older nonvolunteers, have fewer functional and physical impairments, overall better health, higher life satisfaction, and less depression. In addition, they attend religious services more frequently and belong to more social organizations. A twenty-five-year National Institute of Mental Health study found that "highly organized activity is the single strongest predictor, other than not smoking, of longevity and vitality."

The National Executive Service Corps (NESC) is another organization that capitalizes on the talent and experience of retirees. It is dedicated to strengthening the management of America's nonprofit organizations, schools, and governments through high-quality volunteer consulting services. Clients include the arts, education, health care, religion and social services as well as local, state, and federal government agencies. The NESC offers management consultant positions for nonprofit groups ranging from the National Football Foundation and Hall of Fame to the New York Philharmonic. It also trains retired engineers and scientists to fill the need for high school science and math teachers. The NESC is another organization that offers some fascinating opportunities for volunteers who want to give something back.

Eleanor Holtzman is a consultant to the NESC and a member of its board of directors. She is the former president and chief executive officer of the organization. I asked Eleanor to tell me how she got involved with NESC.

"I retired from a four-decade career in marketing and strategic planning in 1992," she said. "I went to the NESC and offered my services. They asked me to create an arts sector servicing the arts community with nonprofit consulting. I did that for six years before becoming president of the organization. The entire experience has been a great challenge and a lot of fun. I love the consulting end of the operation, and I especially love helping other retirees with their life paths. I think the key thing is reinforcing your identity and sense of self-worth. The midlife crisis is nothing compared to the retirement crisis. My hat is off to those who have planned for a gratifying retirement, but that's not the majority. I love helping the rest because I know better than most how fantastic retirement can be.

"I was never a CEO in business; my generation of women was the advance guard of women executives. A few, like Mary Wells and Charlotte Beers, made it to the top, but not too many of us became CEOs. I became a CEO in my retirement. I got to fulfill a lifetime ambition."

A lifelong dream achieved in retirement in a volunteer position: That's Eleanor Holtzman's story. What a waste to think about other important challenges not met by talented older Americans because they haven't entered the world of volunteerism. As early as 1963, President John F. Kennedy decried the "wall of inertia" that stands between seniors and the needs of their communities. His brother Bobby mourned the waste of "millions of older and retired people whose reservoir of skill and experience remains untapped."

Programs such as the Retired Seniors Volunteer Program, the National Senior Service Corps, and Meals on Wheels, to name only a few, have served and been staffed by older Americans. The need is tremendous. Day care centers, public schools, community libraries and youth centers, homeless shelters, public health agencies, nonprofit arts and cultural organizations, hospitals and literacy centers —

all need the wisdom, experience, talents, and skills of older volunteers. Now more than ever before, our actions will impact on the future of our country. Choosing not to volunteer is a powerful choice, with far-reaching negative outcomes for our society. We fulfill our own prophecies and create the world that we've designed by our actions or the lack thereof.

Alexander (Ian) Smith, chairman and CEO of Marsh & McLennan, has been devoted to the protection and enhancement of Central Park for twenty-five years. He was one of the founders of the Central Park Conservancy, which has evolved into an established organization with over five hundred members. With retirement, Ian plans to serve as chairman and devote even more time. "It's a way of giving back," he said. "And at this juncture, what I think the Conservancy needs is something I can do."

Don't wait for retirement to volunteer. Most elderly volunteers are just young volunteers who grew older. Volunteer to stay healthy. Volunteer to stay useful. Volunteer to remain active. Volunteer to demonstrate your personal commitment to a cause. Volunteer to reinforce your religious beliefs.

Volunteer to feel good. Volunteer to give something back. There's no end to the problems society faces, and will continue to face. Every time one does a good deed — we Jews call it a mitzvah — the better you like yourself. Looking in the mirror to see if you like the person you see is not a onetime thing. You shave or apply makeup every day, and you should ask yourself about the person you see in the mirror daily.

On the subject of giving back, Steve Fitzgerald of New Directions had a wonderful story: "My dad drove a bus. He started with trolley cars and he ended up with a bus, and he drove through Harlem his whole career. And what he used to do is run a raffle every year for the bus drivers, and he used to raffle off a hundred dollars and he'd charge five-for-a-dollar tickets, and they'd buy it and he used that money and just gave it to the high school, because they were in need way back then.

"See, someone with my father's skill base, you'd say, well, what is a bus driver going to give back? He used to enjoy training new bus drivers, but there are so many little things they can do, and there's people at every level that can give back — every level. Say you're a bus driver or something and you had a place and you always liked gardening. You could help the botanical gardens. There are a million different things you can do."

Four

NEVER STOP LEARNING:

Educating Yourself and Others

I'll tell you the kind of guy my father was. When I was a little kid, if I asked him a question he didn't know the answer to, he would take his lunch hour the next day and get the answer at The New York Public Library. That evening at dinner, he'd say, "You remember what you were asking me last night? Well, here's the answer." I never knew about his visits to the library until many years later. You can see he was quite a remarkable guy.

C. Everett Koop

The late, great Katharine Graham, who passed away in the summer of 2001 after suffering a fall while at a conference in Sun

Valley, was an inspiration to so many people. The amazing thing about her was, when faced with a challenge of seemingly insurmountable proportions, she didn't run from it: She learned how to do it. As she told me in an interview the year before she died, "I found myself in the deepest water in the middle of the current; there was no going back. When I first took over *The Washington Post* in 1963, everyone thought I would get remarried, and that would be the end of it. But I didn't view this as an alternative to anything. What I felt was enormous responsibility, and I became absorbed by the challenge. I was trying to learn all the time. And I loved what I was doing. You've got to go on learning forever. Never stop. You've never learned enough."

Katharine Graham's own retirement was hardly retiring. She brought the same passion and dedication to her post–*Washington Post* years. "You shouldn't wait until you retire to get interested in your community," she said. "There are so many problems in the country that need attending to. Volunteerism is nonexistent in most countries except here, and I think there's a great deal of good that volunteers can do: Helping families or the homeless or whatever the problem is, an intelligent volunteer can help. I think it is something people should start doing before they retire, and then continue."

Among Ms. Graham's many engagements was her commitment to making a contribution to the betterment of education in Washington. As she said, simply and poignantly, "I want to give back to a world that's been very generous to me."

MUCH TO LEARN, MUCH TO TEACH

If you don't learn, you're finished.

Philip Johnson, Architect

The Third Act is a great time to learn something new, and a great time to share what you've spent a lifetime learning with others. Learning and teaching are in many ways two sides of the same coin — a coin of high value to all concerned.

The other side of that coin is sharing your career expertise with others who value your acquired knowledge. Sometimes in today's high-tech world, expertise is associated with the young, tech-savvy workers. This shortsighted approach overlooks the wealth of experience instilled in those who have been at it for a few decades longer. What a pity to waste the wealth of experience, history, relationship savvy, and general knowledge that we've amassed through long careers.

Sharing this acquired knowledge is a gift to younger workers as well as to those doing the sharing. There is, unfortunately, a high suicide rate among males, especially Caucasian males over seventy-five who feel isolated and unneeded. After a lifetime of gaining knowledge and honing their skills, they disengage from society and gradually come to believe that no one cares, that they no longer make a difference. The experts agree that the antidote for this unfortunate situation is doing something of value for someone else. Sharing wisdom with others is the surest way of reestablishing a sense of purpose and a reason to get out of bed in the morning.

An interesting example of the learning/ teaching ethic is Dr. Victor Grann, noted oncologist and now public health expert. Victor is married to Phyllis Grann, an extraordinary woman in her own right and the former president and CEO of Penguin Putnam Inc. When the Granns were visiting my wife and me a few years ago,

Victor was studying at the Columbia University School of Public Health with the intention of making a career change, a switch from surgery to public health. He was sixty-two when he went back to school to learn a whole new discipline. It sounded like an interesting Third Act story.

"I never wanted to be an old doctor in practice," Victor explained. "After years working at the hospital, I started getting interested in other ways of looking at health, especially public health issues like health outcomes and the cost-effectiveness of hospital procedures. It seemed like a good time for a change, so I enrolled in Columbia University night school."

Soon, Victor decided to quit his practice and matriculate full-time. "It was fun being in school with young people. Most of the people I work with now are quite young — in their twenties and thirties. It's a treat to be with them. They value my age and expertise, and I really hook into their curiosity and their vigor. I've collaborated on several papers with a terrific kid at Columbia who was in a lot of my classes, and I'm teaching a quality-of-life course that has been very exciting."

In the last few years, over a half million Americans over the age of fifty have returned to school, attending local colleges and universities. It's never too late to learn something new, and college towns have become choice retirement spots for elders seeking education, cultural events, seminars, sporting events, and the atmosphere surrounding a mixed-generation living and learning environment. Many universities are already offering "College at Sixty" programs geared toward silver students. (Fordham University and The University of North Carolina were two of the first institutions to create these burgeoning programs.) Another take on this trend is run by the Boston-based Elderhostel, which arranges for seniors to travel to college campuses to live in dormitories and take classes. Continuing education in the Third Act is a boon to health and enjoyment of life.

A big part of late-life education for those of my generation has involved new technology. Mike Wallace laughed heartily as he told of his own and colleague Morley Safer's struggles with the computer. "Neither of us was doing very well with the computers," he said. "We were used to the typewriter. In fact, we both used manual typewriters. All of a sudden, Morley decided, 'God damn it, I'm going to do it!' So he paid three thousand dollars up front to have somebody come in and teach him, nine o'clock every morning. Third week I walk in here and he's standing in the door of his office and he's throwing out the manual typewriter. 'I finally, by God, learned how to do it!' It took me longer to learn, but I did as well."

C. Everett Koop is another one who mastered the new technology — out of necessity. "I'll tell you," he laughed, "when the computer came along, I figured if I keep my head down and don't look, it'll go away and I'll die before anybody says, 'Make that thing work for you.'

"But coincident with my coming up here to New Hampshire, the Department of Commerce put out a request for proposals for things that they wanted to do to stimulate the commerce of the Internet, so I applied for a grant and I got $50 million. My idea was that if patients are going to take charge of their own health, there's no prescription more valuable than knowledge, and one way to guarantee that is to establish an electronic medical record that each patient owns and controls — instead of it being controlled by some insurance company or some hospital or some clinic that says, 'This is our property: Keep away.' And so we founded a little company, two of my friends and I, called Patient Medical Record, Inc., and when we got into the business of trying to really make a record work, we realized we needed people to work it with, so we had to build a little Web site, and we call that Dr. Koop's Community. Well, pretty soon Dr. Koop's Community was bigger than the medical record and we realized that what we're doing is what I wanted to do all my life and that is empower people to make decisions, and so we changed the name of our company to Empower Health, Inc. And then when it became obvious that the real future of health care in this new world of communications was going to be on the Web, then we put it on the Internet."

I marveled at this story. Dr. Koop proves it's possible to go from computer illiteracy to mastery.

LIFTING OTHERS UP

Learning and teaching are both important parts of my daily life. I am able to use and share my previous knowledge and combine all that with my new passion in order to influence others and help make positive changes in health care.

C. Everett Koop

We have to recognize that computer literacy is going to be the key to success in business, teaching, the professions — and inner-city kids are way behind. Something must be done to remedy the situation. Steve Fitzgerald stresses the value of education and encourages his clients to become involved with school districts in need. He has dedicated his time, efforts, and considerable talents to rebuilding and recreating Rice High School in Harlem as an example of the difference a state-of-the-art education can make in the lives of struggling teens.

Rice High School, whose composition is 96 percent black, 3 percent Hispanic, and 1 percent Asian, didn't even have a chemistry lab. Steve got Pfizer to donate $240,000 to put a chemistry lab in the basement. Thanks to his enthusiastic efforts, the school is being rebuilt with modern science and computer labs and new gymnasium facilities — a complete overhaul. Steve's contagious enthusiasm has infected individuals and businesses that have also been major contributors to the project. In 1999, fifty-eight of the fifty-nine graduates went on to college. "This is a fantastic part of my life," Steve said. "I recommend it to all my clients. The rewards are amazing."

Steve added that anyone can make a contribution to education — *anyone*. As an example, he told the story of his mother's ninetieth birthday. He sent out invitations to a surprise party, and told the celebrants not to bring gifts but to bring donations to a scholarship in his mother's name. He then found a young man who needed help. He was studying law, but lack of funds had him working full-time plus weekends to make ends meet. The scholarship enabled this young man to become a lawyer.

My daughter-in-law Lisa Belzberg has been involved in creating a program called "Principal for a Day," which is a wonderful vehicle for matching older, experienced professionals with young minds eager to learn. This program encourages CEOs to adopt a public school and encourage employees to lend their time and talents to the students of that school. Seagram's adopted school is PS 198 in New York City at the corner of Ninety-fifth and Third Avenue. Our employees, especially retired employees, are intimately involved with the school, its students, and the future of both. The give-and-take between students and volunteers has forged some strong bonds and unusual friendships. The project is making a difference in the lives of all involved.

Jane Thompson, architect and city planner, will continue to work at her firm, Thompson Design Group, but she is recasting her role. In addition to running the firm and guiding the work, she sees her role as a bridge and a mentor to her younger associates.

"There are young energetic people who don't know what I know, who have not been where I have been, who haven't met the fascinating figures like Walter Gropius and Frank Lloyd Wright and I. M. Pei whom I have had the great good luck to know. I want to share all of this with them.

"Some days I feel like Methuselah. One of the young people in the office will quote from a story that they read in a textbook, and I'll have to intervene. 'That's not quite it. Let me tell you what really happened. You see, I was there.'

"I can now give more time to projects that need my talents on a volunteer basis.

I'm busier than ever. I will always find some area of usefulness within this framework."

ADDICTED TO LEARNING

I used to think of people's minds as closed elevator doors, and if you could just open them a little bit, then you'd open their receptivity to learning.

Matthew Barrett

Perhaps the strongest advocate for education I met during the interview process was Matthew Barrett. At the time of the interview he was CEO of the Bank of Montreal, but he was poised to retire. He has since become CEO of Barclays, Britain's largest bank. He was also a Seagram director and chairman of the audit committee. What's amazing is that he is entirely self-taught.

Matt's lifelong passion for creative self-education began inauspiciously in his class at school in Ireland, where he ignominiously ranked lowest in his class. Whether or not this was the catalyst for change, Barrett has never looked back as he cut a wide swath through international banking circles, reinventing much of modern banking as we know it. His passion for educating himself and everyone else in his line of sight is legendary.

Describing his young self, Matt said, "I wouldn't have characterized myself as ambitious. I was kind of drifting: I wanted to be a writer, I didn't want to work. But I stayed at the bank and I was pretty good at it, because it wasn't all that complicated. I enjoyed the people side of it. You had to deal with customers, you had to deal with fellow employees. You see all elements of the human condition when you're dealing with people's money, both the good and the bad. So the writer in me — if you like, the amateur writer in me — found the experience much more interesting than I had expected.

"In 1967, I was invited to transfer to Canada. I discovered that you didn't have the lack of opportunities you had in the U.K. or in Europe at that time. If you worked at it, you could pretty well achieve anything you wanted to achieve. As an immigrant I noticed that the natives took everything for granted, so I'd work twice as hard. At that exact time I decided to become an autodidact, to make up for the fact that I hadn't gone to university. I would exploit my colleagues who knew an awful lot more about everything than I did, be it banking or whatever in the textbooks I was cracking. I developed good relationships with them and they were happy to help me."

His secret to success was to volunteer for the jobs nobody else wanted.

He told his superiors that they had nothing to lose by assigning him to those jobs, and he was successful at turning around problem branches. The bank kept giving him tougher and tougher assignments, until he became the CEO.

"One of the innovations I championed was An Institute of Learning, because I had two theories. One was that business is not all that complicated, you can teach it to almost anybody. An awful lot of it is just common sense, and craft, and you can teach craft skills to people. The other is that I got so much from self-education, I wanted as many employees as possible [to do so as well] — even very junior ones who might not have had the advantage of being able to have that kind of experience. Then I brought in visiting professors from various disciplines. I would bring in interesting speakers from around the world to spend lunch and maybe an afternoon with the senior team. He might be an anthropologist or a great demographer. He didn't have to have anything to do with the bank. I used to think of people's minds as closed elevator doors, and if you could just open them a little bit, then you'd open their receptivity to learning."

When I asked Matt about his plans for the Third Act, he told me, "It seems to me that you should divide your time three ways: into work, humanitarian pursuits, and sheer pleasure. I have a friend who's a psychiatrist, and she recommends putting care of the soul on that list. When you're trying to make your way, and you're scratching and clawing to get on in the world, you don't give much time or attention to the child within yourself. I think she'd advise us all to make that number four."

Matthew Barrett is a fascinating human being. It's obvious to me that he won't have idle time when it comes to his Third Act.

Fritz Jacobi spent a lifetime working in public relations, first at National Educational Television, the organization that preceded the formation of PBS, and then as director of public relations at the Columbia Business School. He was forced to retire in his early seventies. The dean of the Business School decided, in Fritz's words, "that he wasn't going to trust anyone over seventy." Fritz continued consulting and freelance writing, but he was restless, and he wanted to do more.

"I remembered that one of my wife's colleagues had years ago helped to found the Public Education Association, which provided volunteer tutors for students in the public school system," he said. "I also knew that public schools here in New York City were understaffed, underbudgeted, and in a state of disarray. It seemed like a worthy outlet for my time and talents. My interest led me to the School Volunteer Program of New York City, Inc., an organization that was founded by three women in the city over forty years ago. Today there are over nine thousand volunteers like me working in elementary, secondary, and high schools throughout the city.

"For the last four years I've worked two mornings each week at Martin Luther King High School at Amsterdam and Sixty-sixth. It's a tough school, a magnet school, and most of the kids are inner-city blacks from other parts of the city. There are also Dominicans, West Africans, Vietnamese, and Malaysians. Lots of these kids are lacking language skills. Some are absolutely brilliant in math and science, but they're having real problems with English. If they can't speak, and they can't write, then they can't get into college. That's where I come in. I've made my living with the Queen's English my whole life. I teach them what I know, and I think I'm making a difference."

Fritz told me about some of his students. He talked about a Malaysian boy of Chinese extraction who was a brilliant science and math student with sub-par English skills. With Fritz Jacobi's help and twenty-three viewings of his favorite film, *Titanic*, "to improve his English," he graduated with top honors and entered college. Another student, a shy Senegalese student, worked long and hard with Fritz. Graduation depended upon English marks, and the English mark depended on completing a final English paper. With Fritz's tutelage he wrote a report on an A. L. Rowse book about Shakespeare, got an 85, passed the course, and went on to college.

Fritz smiled and said, "That's what makes the whole thing worthwhile. I get so much back from these kids. I learn so much from them. And I think what I'm doing is important. I suspect there are many retirees who would love to help others, especially younger people who could benefit from their wisdom. Take a page from my book. I needed more structure and activity in my life, so I started looking for an outlet. I found one that helps me and, even better, helps young people to succeed. It's a very rewarding thing."

David Kearns, ex-CEO of Xerox and now chairman emeritus of New American Schools, is a well-known education activist. He served as deputy secretary of education to President George Bush, and is coauthor with James Harvey of *A Legacy of Learning*, a provocative analysis of the American education system. David has very definite views on learning, which he expressed to me in an interview.

"My interest in education was piqued while I was still at work at Xerox, traveling around the world," he told me. "I wondered why other countries seemed to be succeeding on some levels that weren't being achieved at home. When I observed the ascendancy of Asian and European students' math and science scores compared to comparable scores in the United

States, I realized that we had an emergency in our school system. We had to improve our education. For everyone. That has led me to my current work. If we don't do a better job of educating a broad range of our society, we aren't going to make it."

I agree with David Kearns that our educational system is lacking. If we don't improve that system across the board, I don't see how we can maintain our preeminent global position. This is a cause of great urgency, and one in which the talents and knowledge of older Americans can be used to great advantage for our young people.

Five

KEEP MOVING:

Fitness Gives You Freedom

I exercise every day, and I can do things a woman one-fifth my age can't do.

Kitty Carlisle Hart

When it comes to health, I was more stupid than most, and more lucky.

I smoked most of my life. I started at fifteen or so, and smoked cigarettes mostly, but pipes and cigars as well. I had checked with my doctor and I could see the lung-capacity line declining over a period of time, until one day he told me that I was going to get emphysema. Dr. William Kahane, an eminent lung cancer specialist, had already told me, "I would rather die of lung cancer than live with emphysema."

My wife, Jan Aronson, who had smoked until she was thirty and then had given it up, was patient with me but hated my smoking. I had tried to stop many times, but obviously I had not wanted to stop badly enough. My motivation was weak. But this time it was different. The daughter of a friend had told me of a doctor who used hypnotism to help people quit smoking. I went to him, spent an hour, and made a tape. As instructed, I played the tape to myself morning and night for ten days. On the eleventh day Jan asked me why I had stopped listening to it, and I first said I didn't know, and then remembered it was a posthypnotic suggestion.

The hypnosis had taken place on a Wednesday afternoon. On Thursday I had four cigarettes at lunch, but none the rest of the day. On Friday morning I lit a cigarette as I went to the toilet, got angry with myself, put it out, and have never again smoked. But I knew that, having quit, I would gain weight, and I had decided that rather than fight that part, I would go to the Vertical Club (not far from the Seagram Building in New York) and try to turn the fat into muscle. I was pathetic. The trainer told me to get on the bicycle

116

and do one minute at 80 revolutions. I could barely do it and was out of breath. But I stuck to both quitting and exercising, and eventually I was able to bicycle for an hour without stopping.

Around this time, my great friend Mark Beckman died in a bicycle accident. He was biking in Central Park and not wearing a helmet. His bike slid out from under him on a wet road made slick by the horse manure. When he fell he hit his head hard. He tried to get up, then collapsed. Mark's death was a great shock to me. I had planned a bicycle trip in France the following September, and I decided to go ahead with it and dedicate it to Mark.

I had first heard about bicycling in France some twenty years earlier. I had been visiting my friends John and Felicia Rogan in Canada's Georgian Bay and I met a man at a cocktail party named George Butterfield. He invited me to speak at Toronto's Canadian Club, a noontime luncheon club, and I had agreed. While chatting, he mentioned bicycling from place to place in France where a vehicle would transport your luggage every day as you bicycled from inn to inn, eating great meals and seeing the glorious countryside. I was returning from a trip to South

America, and I suddenly remembered that conversation, and I asked Bill Friedman to check out the situation. George was the Butterfield of Butterfield & Robinson, who are now famous for their biking, hiking, and various other trips throughout the world. We booked a trip that September, and that began an eleven-year annual bicycle trip to France. We have been to different parts of Burgundy and the Loire Valley, to Cognac (where Seagram's subsidiary Martell owns a beautiful château). We've been to Bordeaux a number of times. It's a delight to meet the châteaux owners of wines we import and to dine at their tables, and we've been to islands off the coast of France and to Brittany.

One note about biking: The concept of eating all you want on a bike trip because of all the exercise you get just doesn't work. You get rid of somewhere in the vicinity of three hundred calories an hour biking, depending on the speed and the difficulty of the terrain. If one bikes for five hours, then one has used an extra 1,500 calories. Eating three big meals a day, with wine at lunch and both cocktails and wine at dinner, will put weight on, not take it off. I always feel happy if, after our annual bike trip, I have neither gained nor lost weight. That means I've had a good time, ate and drank well, and exercised enough!

The benefits of the healthy changes I've made in my lifestyle are tremendous. My strength and endurance are up, my weight is down, and, if I do say so myself, I look better than I have in twenty years. I admit to liking the way I look in a mirror. I recount my lifestyle saga because it is, in large part, the story of so many of us in the Third Act. Smoking, eating too much fat, and inactivity are the three major contributors to poor health and a diminished quality of life for all of us. Eighty percent of the health problems of older adults are lifestyle-related and can be eased, postponed, or even eliminated by healthy lifestyle changes.

Studies show that chronic illness and debilitation are not the inevitable end of life if we make good lifestyle choices along the way. Choices concerning exercise, diet, smoking, drinking, and mental challenges are the "building blocks" of old age. And as ye sow, so shall ye reap. In the words of Gerald Brennan, "Old age takes away from us what we have inherited, and gives us what we have earned."

Exercise is the cornerstone of longevity.

According to an extensive ten-year MacArthur Foundation study on aging, "Physical activity is at the crux of successful aging, regardless of other factors."

Exercise can reduce the risk of diabetes, arthritis, and even some cancers. At any age, exercise can increase stamina, balance, strength, and feelings of self-esteem that counteract depression — one of the great killers of the elderly.

Let's face it, though: Lifting weights can be boring. Think of how busy all the gyms get right after New Year's Day, and of the resolutions, and how they revert to normal by the first of February if not before. In all honesty, I can't say I like working out. There are ways, however, to make it more fun. I work out with a trainer. We have a well-equipped room at the office, and after a workout I reward myself by going back to the executive offices on the fifth floor. There I have a steam facility, as well as a whirlpool bath, a sun machine, and a sauna. I typically will take fifteen minutes of sun and ten minutes of steam; then I get into the whirlpool bath, where the temperature is a cool 80 degrees. I do this because if I don't cool down sufficiently, I tend to perspire into the day, and that's a drag. Total immersion is a much better way to cool down for me than a cold shower, which I take after the whirlpool.

Some caution should be taken about weight lifting. It's certainly preferable to get a trainer — a good one. The risk of serious injury is high if one is playing with heavy weights incorrectly. Then, too, one gets a lot more out of an exercise by doing it properly. My trainer in Sun Valley, Peter Anderson, is really strict and insists on proper form. It's incredible how much more I get out of a workout with him. He is also insistent on bending the knees to pick up the weights and keeping the back straight — a classic injury-prevention technique. Another advantage of weight lifting is that it increases bone density, making it less likely that you will break bones in the event of an accident.

My friend Sam Grossman came through a nasty biking accident in Hawaii last year with only a few cuts and bruises, largely because he is in such good shape. Sam's doctor attributes his strong bones to regular exercise and weight lifting. Sam was also wearing a helmet. That's a no-brainer, pun-fully intended. Without a helmet, a simple head-over-heels cycling injury is more likely to be very serious or fatal. Get a helmet and wear it. Who cares if it looks ungainly or terrible? It will protect you in case of an accident!

My trainer educated me. He told me that it's important for older people to work on endurance as well as muscle mass, although strength and endurance do seem to go together. Do more repetitions with lighter weights rather than struggling to lift heavier weights for the sake of bragging rights. This plan is also key for injury prevention, as is good form and controlled speed in both directions. For example, several studies with subjects over age fifty have shown more than three pounds of new muscle following three months of strength exercise. Research has also revealed associated benefits, including increased metabolic rate, more bone mass, lower blood pressure, better blood lipid profiles, greater glucose utilization, improved digestion/elimination, reduced low back pain, decreased arthritic discomfort, and enhanced self-confidence.

Women also need to perform weight-bearing exercise. Lifting weights is a way of building bone density, a prerequisite to fighting osteoporosis. My wife, Jan, does exercise every day, whether it's swimming almost two miles in the morning or lifting weights at the gym. In Virginia and Sun Valley, where we have places, she adds tennis to her list of sporting activities. She's in marvelous shape. Aerobic exercise is also very important. One's heart needs exercise to stay healthy.

Running or bicycling on a daily basis is good for one's heart and one's endurance. I grew cautious about running in New York City. The pavement is hard, which can do damage to one's joints — ankles and knees — and breathing exhaust fumes is not particularly healthy. I now do my aerobic exercise on an indoor bike. I used to like to ride occasionally in Central Park, but the rising number of roller bladers has made that a bit hazardous.

I have found over time — and with a good deal of experimentation — that three one-hour weight-bearing workouts each week works best for me. I also use a stationary bike each morning before breakfast for thirty minutes to improve my aerobic fitness. The benefits of both are measurable and rewarding.

My father always lectured us about moderation — to the point where one day I told him that to be consistent, one had to be moderate in one's moderation. I then ducked the kick I knew was forthcoming.

But he was right: Don't overdo weight lifting or aerobics. The heart needs exercise, not exhaustion. When one has achieved satisfactory goals in weight lifting, it's a very good idea to go on a maintenance regime; just stay fit now that one has gotten there.

Health clubs are realizing that it isn't just twenty- and thirty-year-olds that are interested in health and fitness. There is a growth industry in the health, vitality, and well-being of Third Acts, based on medical breakthroughs, healthier lifestyles, and a bottomless well of interest in the discretionary dollars of older Americans.

According to Wayne L. Westcott, Ph.D., an advisory board member of the Senior Fitness Association and the author of *Building Strength and Stamina* and *Strength Training Past 50*, a person's functional ability is only marginally related to one's age. "I have tested forty-year-olds who function more like twenty-year-olds, and others who function more like sixty-year-olds," notes Dr. Westcott, who believes that there is a twenty-year plus or minus effect associated with one's level of physical fitness. In other words, a dedicated seventy-year-old can achieve the physical conditioning of a fit fifty-year-old.

Studies show that it's never too late to begin a fitness program that includes aerobics, flexibility, and weight-bearing exercises. Increased muscle mass, endurance, strength, and vitality are the rewards. If you started early in life, you're ahead of the game.

DR. KOOP WEIGHS IN

We're the fattest nation in the world, ever. In history.

C. Everett Koop

According to C. Everett Koop, "Studies have shown that changing a sedentary life into one of appropriate exercise can bring real health benefits, even in the tenth decade of life. When I left government, my wife and I specifically bought a three-story town house to help keep us fit. I did at least twenty flights up and down in the course of my daily activity, and that's excellent exercise. I'll be eighty-four in October 2001, and I've been experiencing angina [a painful decrease of blood to the heart muscle] for about nine years. I don't let that stop me. I may not walk as fast as I once did, but I pace myself, and I make it count.

"If you're concerned about your own health — and you should be — then you need to take charge of your health and get yourself fit for the future. There is no prescription that I can give you that is more valuable than knowledge. My entire life has been charted to empower patients through knowledge to take charge of their health."

Exercise may be the most important component of a fit Third Act, but a healthy diet is a key element as well. Experts advise us to lose the "empty" calories — alcohol, sweets, and junk foods. We're also urged to avoid the "cookies and tea" diet that many Third Acts drift into, especially when cooking and eating alone. You are responsible for your own physical fitness, and a healthy diet is necessary to achieve that goal. Go for nutrient-dense foods — fruits, vegetables, lean meat, fish, nuts, and whole grains. I run a bison operation in Virginia because bison meat is so lean and almost cholesterol-free, and tastes terrific. I've learned that the foods that are best for me satisfy me more and taste best. I also take daily vitamin supplements with the encouragement of my doctor. Older women may want to check with their physicians on the wisdom of adding calcium supplements and vitamin E to their daily routine.

Dr. Koop is very disturbed about obesity in the United States. In fact, he told me that if he had served another term as surgeon general, he would have attacked obesity with the same passion with which he took on tobacco smoking. "Even though you never see *obesity* on a death certificate, more than 300,000 Americans died last year because of obesity. It's obvious that living long and living overweight don't go together. I don't meet very many elderly people who are obese, do you?

"We're the fattest nation in the world, ever. In history," Dr. Koop told me, and I agreed with him that this is a crisis. Dr. Koop explained, "I wanted to do something about the crisis of obesity. So in 1996, with the cooperation of then first lady Hillary Rodham Clinton, and using the White House as a backdrop, I pulled together some of the top obesity specialists in the world and we founded Shape Up America! It wasn't a shame campaign, where we said, 'Listen, you fat slob, you've got to get 40 pounds of lard off of you.' Instead, we said, 'Lose a few pounds, be a little more active, see how well you feel, and then do it again.'

"So, what's stopping us? Our research showed that many people — especially older people — didn't exercise because they thought it had to be rigorous to make any difference. Then there were practical barriers, such as lack of access to facilities. One of the goals of Shape Up America! was to elevate walking to a national priority. You don't need equipment to walk. You don't need special facilities to walk. It doesn't cost anything."

THE FITNESS ROUNDTABLE

If there is one theme that all of my interviewees uniformly agreed on, it was exercise and fitness. Let me share their personal thoughts and techniques.

Jimmy Carter's agonized look is one we all remember — captured in print — when he was exhausted running when he was president. That was obviously an exception. He is now seventy-five years old, and here is what he said about his exercise routine. . . .

"I ran this morning. My wife and I ran three miles this morning. We were at the

U.S. Open in New York, and Saturday morning we also ran four miles. We play a lot of tennis. In fact, last week we happened to be home, which is rare, and we played tennis probably five times that week. We have a court behind our house and we're kind of tennis fans.

"We also ski together. The first time I ever saw skis I was sixty-two years old. We climb mountains on occasion. We've climbed Mount Kilimanjaro and we've climbed Mount Fuji. We've climbed up above base camp on Mount Everest. We enjoy doing that. We've become bird-watchers in our older age. We're avid fly fishers. But the point is, we do things together. We both fly-fish, we both climb mountains, we both play tennis, we both ski, and it keeps us together closely."

Bert Fields, renowned entertainment lawyer who recently took up the tango, told me, "Fitness is tremendously important. Don't just sit there and get out of shape. Reading is wonderful, but it can't become your only waking activity. It's no way to spend the rest of your life. Keep moving. Don't just sit there and vegetate. My wife and I play tennis and walk across the city every Sunday. We also swim regularly. Physical fitness promotes mental fitness.

"My father was a surgeon. A wonderful, vital man. Then he retired. Six months later he was an old man. He didn't have a plan, and he didn't stay active. He just sat around the house. Soon he stopped shaving, then he wasn't getting out of his bathrobe, and before he knew it he had became a stooped old man."

Ian Smith, retired CEO of Marsh & McLennan, is now chairman of the Central Park Conservancy. A lifelong running and exercise routine may have lured him into the work of his Third Act.

"I live on Central Park and Sixty-sixth Street, and have done so for twenty-five years," he told me. "Central Park is a very important part of my life. It's almost impossible to conceive of New York without Central Park, or my life without it. I have dedicated myself right now to the preservation and improvement of this amazing resource. Would my life have taken this turn if I didn't run in the park every morning? Who knows?"

Mike Wallace is a longtime proponent of a healthy diet. "Long before anyone talked about it, I had a very healthy diet. Nuts, fruits, vegetables, fish — all natural foods. My then wife, whom I adored for twenty-eight years, insisted on it, and I think it has served me well. I'm in pretty good shape today as a result of it. I've lived in a five-story town house with no elevator for twenty-eight years. Up and down twenty times a day for twenty-eight years is a lot of exercise. Other than that, I do some stretching exercises and play a little tennis."

Philip Johnson, the lord of bountiful longevity, reports that "I get between nine and ten hours of sleep each night. I go to bed at 8:30, and get up at 6:00 or 6:30 — if I oversleep. For the first time in my life I'm actually paying attention to my health. I even exercise a couple of times every week. Previously, I couldn't so much as lean over without toppling. I can lean over now. That's kind of fun."

Elizabeth Murray, the artist, is also a firm believer in exercise. "I am naturally thin, and I get a lot of exercise working. Painters do a lot of physical work just standing and reaching and painting. Staying fit has always been important to me."

Walter Cronkite is naturally active. "Extreme exercise has never been an objective of mine. I sail, of course, but my version of sailing is to man the wheel and issue orders. I like playing tennis; I play often in the summer. I asked my doctor recently if I'd be able to play singles tennis, and he said I could. That made me very happy, since I haven't played in five years."

Kitty Carlisle Hart extends her mental discipline to the physical, and always has. "I exercise every day. I get on the floor and do things a woman one-fifth my age can't do. Now, don't imagine it: You've got to do it."

Arthur Schlesinger: "I've been corrupted by exercise; I depend on it. I rise and do five miles on my stationary bike while listening to NPR. Then it's breakfast with my wife — grapefruit juice, cinnamon toast, and plain yogurt, followed by the *Herald Tribune* and *The Times*. That's how I start every day." As for the end of the day: "I abhor the fashion that spread through America in the eighties and nineties of replacing cocktails with white wine. A glass of sauterne is hardly what the organism requires after a hard day."

The message is loud and clear. Diet and exercise are both critical and crucial elements of a healthy and vital Third Act. The good news is that a healthy lifestyle is tremendously rewarding, reasonably easy to accomplish, never too late to implement, and fun. Dare I say that? It's just fun? Have we lost our capacity for play because we've aged? Absolutely not. Being fit is fun. Feeling good is fun. Looking good is fun. Physical and mental acuity is fun. And fun is precisely what we need to encourage in all of us, both young and old. The French call it *joie de vivre*. The joy of life. Am I for it? Absolutely.

Six

VITAL CONNECTIONS:

Maintaining a
Personal Support Network

My father always used to say that when you die, if you've got five real friends, then you've had a great life.

Lee Iacocca,
Former Chief Executive Officer, Author

Connection. One of Webster's first definitions is "the relation of people or things that depend on, involve, or follow each other." That definition covers a wealth of possible connections available to all of us throughout our lives, but the connections we maintain and nourish in our Third Act are the most important of all. It is critical to stay connected to family, friends, colleagues, neighbors, church members, and club members.

Frequent visits with friends and frequent attendance at organization meetings and social gatherings are proven to be harbingers of well-being in later life.

The world has changed since I was a boy. Life no longer revolves around the family. Children move far away to start careers and follow opportunities. Visits become infrequent, and relationships hinge on phone calls and E-mail messages — if you're lucky. Many seniors settle into a lonely existence that destroys the bonds of connection that have invigorated their lives. Too many older Americans turn their interest and absorption inward, where it no longer revitalizes or adds zest to life. Watching television and worrying about your health is not the recipe for an exciting Third Act. It is necessary to nourish the standing connections and reach out and make new ones.

I can't overemphasize the rewards that can come from friends and family. But closeness shouldn't mean dependence. If you are counting on spending lots of time with your grandchildren after you retire, you may be in trouble. While it is true that grandchildren and grandparents have a common enemy, that flimsy alliance doesn't work as the grandchildren get older and the parents have their own busy lives. That doesn't mean that one should avoid having great relationships with one's family; I'm just saying you can't depend on them to fulfill you. You always have to find that fulfillment in yourself.

Having said that, friends and family are important in one's life. I have a large family — seven children: Sam, Edgar, Holly, Matthew, Adam, Sara, and Clare. I also have twenty-two grandchildren. My youngest two children by my second wife, Sara and Clare, aged twenty-five and twenty-two, have not started having children, so there may be more to come. My children are somewhat scattered: Two families are on the West Coast, two are in New York City, and one is in Charlottesville, Virginia. My daughter Clare is intent on becoming an Olympic rider (show jumping), and her older sister is devoting her time to going to school, helping organize the horses, and all the other complicated details that go along with that sport. Many of my grandchildren are having their Bar and Bat Mitzvahs now, so the family gets together regularly. Often we have a family reunion in Sun Valley, Idaho, where I have a home, and it's great fun watching the various cousins of different ages interact.

I don't make the mistake my father made of insisting on loving all the children the same. I love all my children, but I acknowledge and respect that they are separate and different children, and my relationship with each of them is thus different. My oldest is Samuel Bronfman II, named after his grandfather in English, and after his maternal great-grandfather in Hebrew. He lives in California, where he is deeply involved in the wine business. My second son was named after me by his mother. When I complained that it would be confusing, she replied that we would call him Gary. Since I had named the first, it was her turn. When Edgar Jr. was perhaps four or five, he insisted on being called Edgar. Many years later, when I asked him why, his answer was that Sammy had five letters; Holly, his younger sister, had five letters, and he wanted to have five letters too.

Holly and I have had an on-again, off-again relationship up until recently, and now we're loving friends. Her choices of men were not very good for her, and she felt I didn't understand her. She got married again to an Israeli in July 2000. He is a very nice young man, and they seem terribly happy together.

I have one brother, Charles, of whom

I'm very fond, and a sister, Phyllis, who lives in Montreal and of whom I'm also very fond. I have a few close friends, and I consider myself a very lucky man.

INDEPENDENCE WITHOUT ISOLATION

Sitting alone doesn't help me. I love to go into the office. If the kids [his colleagues], aren't there I'm furious.

Philip Johnson

The redoubtable Beverly Sills made an excellent point when she told me, "When I grew up, *community* meant knowing your next-door neighbor. In those days *community* meant people, as opposed to today, when it too often means facilities. We lived in an apartment, but we always knew all the neighbors in the building. It was just unthinkable not to know who lived next door or underneath us. The word *community* meant people."

Connection is no longer automatic. Several generations of families no longer live under the same roof or in the same town or even on the same coast. Nurturing a community and remaining connected require some effort on our part these days.

Renowned contemporary artist Elizabeth Murray offered some interesting insight on "aloneness" after the nest empties.

"I had a son in my twenties who is now a wonderful man in his thirties; then I remarried and had two children in my forties," she said. "This has definitely had a major effect on my take on aging. Now the girls are in their late teens and will soon both be away at college. I have to tell you, I'm really looking forward to it. For the first time in my life I'll just be able to *work*. I'm very excited about it, but I recognize the need for caution. I think I could easily isolate myself too much from people. Socializing, conversing, connecting face-to-face, is very important as you get older."

Studies show that loneliness and isolation can be more detrimental to good health than bad habits, such as smoking or not exercising. Too many of my peers have spent a working lifetime looking forward to a retirement that is defined by inactivity. They stop taking that extra step and making that extra effort. Soon the circle of their lives has dwindled, and they find they are very unhappy with this new backseat view of life.

The can-do attitude that characterized the first two thirds of their lives — the learning and earning years — has dried up and gone south! Society has imposed an unacceptable and unrealistic model of postretirement that designates a Third Act lacking involvement, creativity, and an adventurous spirit. *Needy, frail, alone,* and *dependent* are words that must be banished from the vocabulary of aging Americans.

My friend Kitty Carlisle Hart is a living, breathing embodiment of those words of wisdom. "I'm out every day and every night, and I'm always put together. I've got my makeup on, my hair done, and I have a nice dress. Whatever else may come my way, I'm up, I'm out, and I look good."

The point is driven home over and over again. A successful Third Act is not defined simply by health versus sickness: Connection and involvement are key ingredients for a vital life. These are the opposites of loneliness, inactivity, boredom, and isolation, which are proven risk factors for poor health. These factors are also leading signifiers of depression, "the great debilitator."

Depression is widely undertreated in older Americans, who suffer from it almost twice as often as the general population. Overmedication, increased stress, loss of friends and possibly your spouse, job loss, and illness are all contributing factors to Third Act depression, which is often dismissed by families and medical professionals as the inevitable toll of growing older. It is not inevitable. It is not natural. It can often be treated.

Mike Wallace is one of the brave ones who has come forward to discuss his battle with — and victory over — depression.

"I think I am a wiser and kinder man for having been through clinical depression," he said. "I really do. That doesn't mean I've lost the edge, but I'm more empathetic, more careful about making snap decisions. I think I like myself better."

Dr. Ira Katz, professor of psychiatry and director of geriatric psychiatry at the University of Pennsylvania in Philadelphia, is an authority on late-life depression and a pioneer in treating it. "Everyone who works with older people is amazed by their ability to cope with disease, loss, disability — as long as they're not depressed," he pointed out.

Dr. Katz's studies have shown that depression turns up the volume on pain, accelerates osteoporosis, and increases other symptoms of disease and ill health. Any suspicion of clinical depression, including the onset of any symptoms of depression, should be discussed with your physician and evaluated for appropriate treatment. Depression can be treated at any age. Avoiding the building blocks of serious depression should be a daily priority in all of our lives. Toward this end, we should actively create the healthy, involved circumstances that discourage the onset of depression. And these include maintaining close relationships with family and friends.

When I asked Mike Wallace what was most important to him at this stage of his life, he answered without hesitation, "Family. Much more than it used to be. My self-absorption was total for a long time."

It's a plain reality that as we age there are going to be times of illness, though — and that means one or the other of a couple is going to end up with the role of caretaker, and possibly the widow or widower. Jane Thompson talked about the next phase of growing old: the need for services. She described a friend of hers, a widower, who was having trouble finding an apartment because he wouldn't be able to cope with the stairs, or with fending for himself. She also talked about what life has been like with her husband, Ben Thompson, a prominent architect, designer and urban planner, since he became ill.

"Besides having a stroke, Ben lost his eyesight," she told me. "After the stroke, he didn't have the use of one hand, and he was having perceptual problems — he had lost most of the use of one eye — but he decided he was going to go back to painting. Very courageous. In the course of a year, he sat in his chair and painted over fifty watercolors. And we said, 'Wow! This is great.' And a small gallery in the Barnstable area, where we have our house, said they'd put on a show, and he sold half the pieces. We were so delighted. We thought now, at last, he had found his rehabilitation. Then within two weeks he had bleeding in his remaining eye and lost the use of it.

"Now his hearing is getting worse and worse. I think that's the hardest thing of all. They say if you lose your sight you lose contact with objects, but if you lose your hearing you lose contact with people. It's very hard to communicate. Now, when I want to have a conversation with him, the best thing I can do is call him on the telephone, and he'll pick up his line with the amplifier and we can really get it straight."

Jane observed that few people are prepared for these life-and-death crises, and few are prepared for how they're going to live after the death of a spouse. She did have one fascinating idea, though. "We don't have the mechanisms in the family or in the community to care for one another as we get older. My mother was Norwegian. They had a big family and took care of everybody. All the stray aunts and uncles who were widowed just moved into Grandmother's house. But what do we do? We could buy a house. A whole bunch of friends could do it — and we've discussed it. When we're all alone, we could have a co-op, like we had at Vassar, and share the cooking and provide companionship."

Maybe Jane is onto something.

Only thirty years ago, doctors were convinced of the validity of something called the disengagement theory. This bit of wisdom involved "letting go" of jobs, friends, hobbies, pleasures, family members, and finally, life itself, as the final fillip in the process of aging. Fortunately, this theory has gone the way of other crackpot ideas, like bloodletting to balance the humors. Today's aging experts stress engagement with every aspect of life as key to maintaining vitality throughout the Third Act. You are never too old to create, to produce, to explore, or to enjoy.

Socialite and philanthropist Brooke Astor danced the night away at her ninety-fifth birthday party. It was a gala event. Brooke told her assembled guests that she would continue to explore life. "There are still so many places in the world that I haven't seen, so many things that I haven't done." The essence of the life force resides in those thoughts. The past generation's sense of limitations has evaporated. If it can be envisioned, it can be accomplished.

Another trend taking root among older Americans is the desire to return to an urban living environment after raising families in suburbia. According to Jane Thompson, who has been a professional city planner for countless years, "People want to move back into cities, especially in their later years. They don't want to be isolated; they enjoy the convenience; they are thrilled to be able to take part in the exciting daily life of a vibrant city. It's a practical solution to a checklist of desires." I was surprised to learn that only 5 percent of Americans over sixty-five are living in nursing homes, and only another 4 percent live in any kind of assisted living or retirement village facility. The majority of older people maintain their independent living situations or create new models of the Third Act lifestyle.

Singles and couples are banding together with like-minded friends and associates to create shared living arrangements that combine the best parts of independent living and community support. We are seeing new models created all the time.

STAY CLOSE TO THOSE YOU LOVE

As long as I have my wife and something to do every day that's challenging, I think I'll be okay.

Bert Fields

The Third Act is an important time to nurture and embrace close family relationships — although this doesn't happen as a matter of course in everyone's life.

I never met a real family like the one on Walton's Mountain. Television has fed us a steady stream of impossibly perfect and loving families. No real-life family could ever measure up to these unrealistic creations; yet, this is the standard that we too often use when measuring our own family's togetherness grade.

According to Katharine Graham, "Families are like the girl with the curl in the middle of her forehead. When she was good she was very good, and when she was bad she was horrid.

"I don't think that all families are wonderful all the time," she said. "Families run uphill, and they run downhill, just like management. All you can hope is to stay the uphill course most of the time."

No matter what crisis she has to face, Jane Thompson depends on the youthful spirit of her grandchildren to keep her going. "We have ten grandchildren," she said. "Five of them are mine and five are Ben's, but they all belong to both of us. They provide a lot of fun and pleasure for us. In fact, they're the best sport of all."

Jimmy Carter also weighed in on his growing family. "Rosalynn and I are the genuine matriarch and patriarch of our family," he said. "There are about twenty of us now — our children, their spouses, and our grandchildren. We make a special effort to keep them close to us and to each other. At least once a year we all go together to some nice place and spend a week, just so our different grandchildren can get to know each other. The family bond is very important."

I thank God every day for my darling, brilliant wife, Jan Aronson. Many of the successful people we interviewed — especially the men — spoke eloquent paeans to their own spouses.

Jimmy Carter unabashedly adores and respects his Rosalynn. "We are full partners in everything. Rosalynn is side by side with me when we negotiate peace, when we monitor an election, when we do everything in life."

Walter Cronkite advised, "One of the things that I would suggest that is helpful is to have a helpful wife. I do — my wife Betsy — and I recommend it."

Dr. Koop told me, "My wife has been my sounding board. I have a little agreement with myself that says listen to her first because she's very wise. Her instincts are sound, and she has an unfailing instinct for what is true."

Mike Wallace pulled no punches. "My best advice? Do what I've done. Marry four times." He admitted he was being a bit facetious, but not entirely. "I'm nobody without a woman," he told me. "I've not been unmarried since I was twenty-two.

Life lived with an interesting companion is an interesting life."

It was Jane Thompson who tickled me most on the subject of marriage, though, when she quoted Charles Eames, who said, "The secret of a long, successful marriage is two separate bathrooms."

Both social support and human contact are essential for sustained function and continued well-being in the Third Act. Friendship supplies them in abundance. Friends, as they say, are God's way of taking care of us.

All of my interviewees valued their close friends and confidants deeply, and most spoke of the delight they found in making new friends in the ranks of the young. It seems it keeps them young at heart. Katharine Graham told me that her thirty-something granddaughter had become one of her dearest friends and allies. "You've got to make new friends as time goes on or you can end up kind of stranded. Luckily I've been able to make younger friends and new friends. But it's not a given; you have to make an effort." She believed that the influx of young ideas kept her in touch with the world at large and added to her love of life.

Philip Johnson, one of the greatest living architects, spoke to me about his work habits and his sources of inspiration. "Sitting alone doesn't help me," he admitted. "I love to go into the office every day, early. It recharges my battery. I am inspired by the interplay of ideas with the young people on my staff. If I get to the office and the kids aren't there yet, I'm furious."

Mike Wallace agrees, "I think it's an excellent idea to surround yourself with young people. I am surrounded by people who are at least twenty-five to thirty years younger than I am. They are extremely helpful to me, and, I trust, I reciprocate. Television is a very collaborative undertaking. There's excitement when different views and ideas are shared."

As is so often the case, historian Arthur Schlesinger had the last word on friends. "I have friends of all ages. After all, my wife is twenty years younger than I am. I have very good friends among the younger historians, and some of my dearest friends, like George Kennan and Ken Galbraith, are sprightly nonagenarians."

Loneliness and isolation create tremendous risk factors for your health — physical and mental. It seems obvious: The mind/body connection is real and definable. Human contact and social support from friends, family, neighbors, and those to whom we extend a helping hand have direct positive benefits on our health. Older Americans with high social support actually have significantly lower levels of stress than those who endure isolation and loneliness.

It's never too late to add new friends to your life. Making new friends in the final third is a pleasure and a sure way to keep your connection muscles flexible. Becoming involved in your church or synagogue committees, civic organizations, or local politics are just a few of the ways to enhance your circle, spark your interest, and increase your holiday card list. It's all about taking that extra step, extending yourself. The effects are immediate, calculable, and beneficial.

Seven

DREAMS CAN COME TRUE:

They're Not Only for the Young

I think the knack is to keep your enthusiasm up because there are so darn many options when you reach sixty-five that you didn't have when you were younger.

David Culver, Investment Banker

"I call it graduation not retirement." David Culver, 75, is the former head of Alcan Aluminum and the current driving force of Culver and Coe, investment bankers. He is already planning his next career move, either playing piano in a cocktail lounge or becoming a professional golf caddy. David Culver should be teaching a master's class on the Third Act. He's a natural.

"It struck me long ago that when we're

twenty-two or twenty-three or twenty-four years old, we graduate from school with tons of enthusiasm and damn few options," he said. "We get a job and usually settle down in the same field — or even the same job — for the next four decades. The tragedy comes when we reach sixty-five and find ourselves with oodles of options but darn little enthusiasm.

"I knew from an early age that the trick was going to be to keep my enthusiasm high. To that end I have always experimented with life by trying new things. I decided to never be afraid of looking stupid or odd. If I get the chance to try anything new, I go for it.

"My first boss, a Swiss scientist in Geneva, asked me two questions when I applied to work for him. First he asked if I had a motto. I didn't but I remembered a quote from *Readers' Digest* that I had read on the 'throne' just that morning. I co-opted it on the spot and answered, 'Nothing in excess, even moderation.' He seemed to accept that, then asked if I knew the three secrets of happiness in life. I had no glib answer for that one and admitted as much. He told me the answer, and I've never forgotten it: 'The first secret is to set reasonable near-term goals. The second, always have an alternative plan. And third, try new things.'

"If you can embrace these principles, age sixty-five can be one of the most exciting times of your life. Set realistic goals, have a plan B, and don't be afraid to try something new."

What a fantastic take on life, especially life in the Third Act. To repeat career counselor Steve Fitzgerald's mantra, "Attitude is everything."

This entire concept of reinventing yourself postretirement is a groundbreaking one. It requires throwing away the negative stereotypes and myths of aging that have been accepted by most as fact. For example:

Myth: Old age equals sickness and mental decline.

Fact: The National Long Term Care Survey, a periodic sampling of 20,000 Americans over sixty-five, continues to show substantial drops in chronic disability rates. More people are living longer and are living healthier. Today there are dramatic differences in the way that older people live and work and play.

Gerontologist Bernice Neugarten, a professor of human development at the University of Chicago, was the first to categorize the "young-old" and the "old-old" based on function, not a number. The "young-old" live and thrive while retaining health and function. The "old-old" experience a loss of function based on disease or disability. The amazing news, wrote Neugarten, is that even in the eighty-five-plus group, more than one third report no limitation due to health.

As for mental decline, according to the MacArthur Foundation Study of Aging in America, "There is no such thing as senility. The view that old age is inevitably accompanied by substantial reduction in mental function is clearly wrong. . . . Growing old for most people means maintaining full mental function." So much for that myth.

Other myths include the delusion that older Americans can't have fun, lack energy, can't memorize, and don't have sex. False on every count.

I think the most dangerous myth of all is that there comes a mysterious birthday when it is no longer possible to make lifestyle changes — the you-can't-teach-an-old-dog-new-tricks birthday.

My interviews put to rest this insidious lie. There is no cutoff date for creative thinking, creative activity, or creative living. The secret is to believe it, to change your perceptions about growing old, to focus on possibilities, to create and realize visions of the future. There is no cutoff date for dreaming or making dreams come true. It's like my grandfather used to say, "If you think you can or you think you can't, you're right."

David Culver thinks he can, and he isn't afraid to take a chance and give it a try. He's already planning for the next chapter of the David Culver story.

"There are two things I've always wanted to do," he told me. "One is to play piano in a little band with time off to play cocktail-hour piano for little old ladies who might be entertained by me. I can imagine doing that. The other thing I would enjoy is being a caddy at a good golf course. It would be a healthy pastime and a fascinating opportunity to observe human behavior at close range. I only hope my legs hold up. There are so many possibilities. I feel like a kid in a candy store."

This is thinking outside the box — way outside the box. In David Culver's mind the box has disappeared. We all need to take this thinking to heart when making plans for the Third Act. When your first career ends, it's necessary to create a new gauge of personal significance and self-worth. Transition times in life are difficult: They require creativity and enthusiasm. Whether you feel like it or not, you've got to move. In the words of nonagenarian track and field star Payton Jordan, "Nothing ever just happens; we have to make it happen."

First-time retirement is a rare opportunity to redirect your energies into something new and exciting. Second, third, and fourth retirements get better. Or so I'm told.

PLAY BALL!

I didn't plan it, but I wished it.

Bob Daly, Dodgers CEO

Some of the most successful second careers spring from a lifelong dream or hobby. Bob Daly has refined Third Act career changes into an art. After decades in the television and movie industries, most notably at Warner Brothers, where he and partner Terry Semel raised the bar on the movie industry's bottom line for over two decades,

Bob Daly decided to follow his bliss.

"After leaving Warner, I realized there was still only one thing that I wanted to do with my life," he said. "I wanted to run the Los Angeles Dodgers. I've always had a passion for baseball and especially for the Dodgers. I grew up in Brooklyn, and I've been a Dodger fan since I was six years old."

Two months after leaving his successful career at Time-Warner, Daly sat down with Rupert Murdoch and proposed a deal to buy an equity position in the team and become chairman, CEO, and managing partner. Murdoch agreed on the spot. It was a very fast negotiation.

I asked Daly if he had planned for this stunning transition in his life. "I didn't plan it, but I *wished* it," he said. "I had a feeling that if I ever went over and met with Rupert, I could accomplish it. I didn't know if I could do it, but I wanted it very badly. To be honest with you, my three oldest children listened to me talk about the Dodgers for so many years, they really believe that I *willed* it to happen.

"All I know is, I made a dream come true. The day I made the press announcement was the happiest day of my life. I've had a building named after me, I've won

Academy Awards, I have my hands and feet in cement at the Chinese Theatre, but that was the happiest day of my professional life.

"Obviously, I'm not making anything compared to what I was making at Warner, but I've been fortunate, and this was not about money. To me this was all about passion. I love what I'm doing."

My hat is off to Bob Daly, who has reinvented himself with passion and enthusiasm. He proves that fairy tales *can* come true — especially for the young at heart. We can learn from his success.

Steve Fitzgerald of New Directions also tells his clients to think outside the box. "Everyone has a variety of talents, not just the ones they used to pay you for the first two thirds of their lives," he pointed out. "You can use what you've done, add the skills you've acquired, and create something new."

Entertainment lawyer Bert Fields has followed that advice in planning his next career move. Following the advice of client Mario Puzo, he wrote two novels — strangely enough, about a lawyer in California. Next he wrote a history book about Richard III, trying to solve the mysterious whodunit murder of the young princes in the Tower.

"I got to do a lot of research in London and all over England. It was great fun, and I decided to continue in that vein from now on," he explained. "I will try to bring skills that I learned practicing law into solving historical problems.

"I've always loved to write, and writing is a large part of being a good lawyer. By applying that skill and the skill of analyzing problems and solving factual disputes, I now find myself solving factual disputes in my books. My next challenge is to take on the question of William Shakespeare's true identity. It will probably take about ten years to research and write. What terrific fun. It's the coming together of many skills in a completely new endeavor, and I love it."

GREAT REVIVALS

I'd like to be a song-and-dance man in my next life.

Walter Cronkite

Kitty Carlisle Hart had not sung professionally for ten years when the head of the Metropolitan Opera lured her back to the stage with an offer to headline the American musical theater portion of a Metropolitan series called "Art New York." When the director suggested that someone else sing the songs as Kitty narrated, she balked and said, "I don't think so."

She threw herself into intensive training, like an athlete, coaxing her voice back into shape. The results have been spectacular — and lucrative.

"I'm singing like a bird again," she said, delighted. "I like to say that I've gone back to my night job, singing and performing all over the country. I've even performed my concert in London.

"I've never had the kind of success I have now. *Never.* People jump up and act as if it were the Second Coming. It's wonderful. I walk down the street, and I just smile all the time.

"Everything I've started in life I started late. Who knows what I am going to be doing when I'm 100?"

Kitty is a real tonic. She's charming, beautiful, and tough as steel. She personifies the can-do factor so necessary in the Third Act. You've got to believe in your ability to handle new situations, solve problems, and succeed. Forget about age;

it's just a number. In the words of André Maurois, "Aging is a bad habit which a busy person has no time to form."

Stay interested, stay curious, learn something new every day. I heard this advice from every successful person I interviewed. Different words, but exactly the same thought.

Dr. Koop agreed: "I learn all the time from everything I do. I never cease to be amazed at the advantages of learning. I think people are blessed with curiosity."

Arthur Schlesinger, who has had a very full and fascinating life, told me, "Yes, I've had a very good time, but I still want to do more. After all, it's not over yet."

Walter Cronkite told me, "I attribute my vitality to a continuing curiosity, which is one of the hallmarks of a journalist — and of successful aging."

There is no question that life can be great in the Third Act. Make it great by experiencing your power, assessing your options, making choices, and getting to work. As Beverly Sills told me, "There are no shortcuts to any place worth going."

Eight

WORDS OF WISDOM:

Lessons Learned in the Third Act

What I essentially did was to put one foot in front of the other, shut my eyes, and step off the edge. The surprise was that I landed on my feet.

Katharine Graham, Wife, Mother,
Newspaper Publisher,
Pulitzer Prize Winner, My Friend

That quote sums up what made Katharine Graham a great woman in all three thirds of her life. Born in 1917, she was the daughter of Eugene Meyer, an industrialist who bought *The Washington Post* in 1933. After she married and had children, her husband, Philip Graham, succeeded Meyer as publisher. Katharine devoted herself to her children, her husband, and her home. Life seemed very linear and predictable until her husband's suicide in 1963. Suddenly — and unexpectedly — Katharine Graham was elevated to publisher of one of the nation's most influential newspapers. She stayed at the helm of *The Washington Post* for thirteen years before handing the reins over to her son Don. During those years she guided her paper through the Watergate crisis, earning her place in history and becoming one of the twentieth century's most influential newspaper people.

In 1998 she won the Pulitzer Prize for her highly regarded memoir, *Personal History.* She followed this triumph with more writing, extensive volunteer and civic activities and work as head of the board's executive committee at her beloved *Washington Post.*

The last time we spoke, she told me in her crisp patrician accent, "Life is like business: You have to try new things at every stage and be prepared to fail. Bromidic though it may sound, sometimes you will fail, which is one of life's terribly difficult lessons. When you do, you pick yourself up and move on."

One foot in front of the other, moving forward, conquering your fears while you conquer new worlds. Katharine Graham's extraordinary life is an example to all that want to succeed in the Third Act.

In the course of my interviews I was exposed to a treasure trove of wisdom from a remarkable group of men and women. Their words are an inspiration. How could anyone observe their spirit or hear their reflections without feeling a rush of energy and a renewed confidence?

Bob Layton, who runs the Senior Lawyers Committee of the New York State Bar Association, told me that those men and women who can make the change, who can leave their egos at the door and enter the new stage with fresh enthusiasm, experience a burst of renewal. They're enervated by their new situation. It takes years off of them. "They're running around in jeans and sport shirts like young Turks making big changes in the lives of those less fortunate," he said. "They understand the endless possibilities of this period in their lives. They are so busy living that they don't seem to have time for aging."

No time for aging. Now that is a red-letter Third Act slogan. Or how about "Old is not a number" or "We are the clockbusters." Ashley Montagu had it all together way back then when he wrote, "The idea is to die young as late as possible." Montagu understood the principles of the Third Act before its time.

Today, seniors want to lengthen not only the life span but also our health, happiness, and productivity spans. We want to live to be 100 or more, and we want to live, love, and enjoy every moment of it. (Gerontologists are speculating that the upper natural range of human life span may be somewhere between 110 and 130!) We want to stay healthy, stay out of nursing homes, and maintain our independence while we're at it.

I asked Philip Johnson — who collaborated with Ludwig Mies van der Rohe in the design and construction of the "Building of the Millennium," the Seagram Building — what piqued his interest most at this point in his celebrated career. Which of his famous projects held him most in its thrall? He leaned across the table without hesitation and said, "What interests me most is the next project I'm doing. And the next one after that. All my attention is focused on the horizon, though I don't know what's on that horizon. But I'll find out. If you don't keep learning, you're finished. The only reality in the world is change. As Heraclitus said, 'Change is the only absolute in life.' Luckily, I love change."

Philip Johnson's spirited enthusiasm for his nonagenarian status delighted and intrigued me. Many of my interviewees held similar views about their venerable ages. In the words of Dr. Thomas Perls, director of The New England Centenarian Study, "People used to say, 'Who would want to live to be 100?' Now they are realizing it's an opportunity."

There's a certain freedom that comes with age. Mike Wallace laughed when he told me, "One of the great things about getting this old is the absolute freedom to say what you want. What the hell? What are they going to do? Fire me? Kill me? I'm fearless."

Mike's colleague, Walter Cronkite, concurred. "I am in a position now to speak my mind. And that is what I propose to do."

Bert Fields told me, "I'm just thrilled with this part of my life. I don't waste a thing. I use every experience, everything I've learned — every skill I possess — in everything that I do. My life is rich. I have my family, I have my practice, and I have my writing. I tell you truly, I've liked every year more than the year before."

★ ★ ★

Success in the Third Act means rejecting the myths and stereotypes of aging that lean toward the frail and needy and away from healthy, involved, and contributory. Ageism, bigotry toward the old, is a cultural prejudice that must be confronted and overcome.

Robert Neil Butler, pioneering gerontologist and founding director of the National Council on Aging, sees ageism as similar to sexism and racism. Butler has been a crusader in this arena for more than forty years, and he uses his vast knowledge and erudite presence to burst the myths that surround aging. Myths that stereotype seniors as "impoverished, impaired, ready for nursing homes, senile, and sexless." He believes the culture has wrongly attributed to age much that is actually a function of disease or social adversity, not aging. In his words, "Disease, not age, is the villain."

And disease is no longer the inevitable companion to aging. According to Dr. Koop, "There are two types of diseases: those that we develop inadvertently and those that we bring upon ourselves by failure to practice preventive measures."

As we've learned, good genes are only a small part of the successful aging process.

More important are close attention to diet and exercise, productive activity, good medical care, and a rich inner and spiritual life. These are the true deciding criteria of a rich Third Act, one that makes a distinction, in the words of gerontologist Harry Moody, between the "wellderly" and the "illderly."

Most of the men and women that I interviewed accepted and, to varying degrees, lived by the diet and exercise imperatives that modern science has decreed necessary for healthful aging. Although they are in the privileged percentile of Americans to whom top-notch health care and medical screening are readily available, they were concerned about a health care system that doesn't offer the same care to all Americans.

Dr. Koop told me, "The ethical imperative for health care reform is more compelling than economic or political pressures. During the last years, when everyone was saying that health care reform was on the horizon, they seemed to have forgotten the definition of *horizon;* it is an imaginary line in the distance which recedes as you approach it." Koop was only one of the interviewees who expressed concern at the state of health care in the United States. Walter

Cronkite said, "America's health care system is neither healthy, caring, nor a system." It is critical that we all dedicate ourselves to solving the health care crisis as well as other social problems in our country.

Every successful person I interviewed spends some time each week "giving back." Jimmy Carter, of course, is a paragon of giving; John Carter Brown gives generously of his time to organizations devoted to the public weal; Katharine Graham's philanthropic projects were legion; former Seagram executive Mel Griffin works with the Salvation Army; Fritz Jacobi teaches English to foreign students; David Kearns is chairman emeritus of the New American Schools and a vital proponent of education reform; Beverly Sills has given tirelessly of her time and talents to her special charities, especially for the deaf. I could go on and on. The list of interviewees is a roll call of volunteerism and civic activism. This component seems to be a linchpin of a successful Third Act.

Vartan Gregorian has long promoted the use of senior talent. "In terms of the needs of an aging America," he said, "they should not sit in front of the television and look at soap operas only, because here is a great reservoir of talent. They can do something about world problems. Why can't there be a kind of retired Peace Corps? In Pakistan, I was on the board of Arahan University in Karachi. They were asking, 'How can we afford to educate doctors to the maximum?' I said, 'Why don't you bring ten retired Nobel laureates every year for one month? Nice hotel, medical facilities, and so forth. Have them teach your medical doctors about the latest techniques. They would love it.'"

Freud said that love and work are the essentials of human life. My research tells me he was right. Whether embarking on a continuation of a long career like Philip Johnson's ongoing architectural work or something completely new like Lillian and Miles Cahn's goat cheese business, all of my interviewees warmed to the subject of their current passions and projects. They came alive, their eyes sparkled, and their faces became more animated when the subject turned to their work. Obviously, productive activity is yet another critical component of the good Third Act.

As for the importance of a loving circle of family and friends, much has been written, and it all appears to be irrefutable.

Frequent interaction with those we love —
and those who love us — is a harbinger of
well-being in the Third Act. We've got to
stay involved with friends, with family,
with colleagues, with younger people who
need our knowledge and our stories.

Or, as a sparkling Kitty Carlisle Hart
shared with me at a Manhattan gala, "Nobody knows the stories I know because I'm
the only one left who knows them. And
I'm going to pass them on."

Hobart Gardiner, the head of International Executive Service Corps, told me,
"The aboriginals in Canada — they call
their Native Americans aboriginals — have
a theory about life. They believe that as
people age, it is their duty to pass their
wisdom on to the younger people. It is an
ethical imperative!" Eleanor Holtzman,
who fulfilled her life's ambition by becoming CEO of the National Executive
Service Corps, expounded on the problems of changing identity when we met.

"I think the key to making a successful
transition to the third phase of life is maintaining your identity, your sense of who
you really are when your life and work
change," she said. "People talk about a
midlife crisis, but I think the life crisis you
experience at retirement is even more in-

tense. You've lost your title and there's no-body hanging on your every word, saying, 'Hey, that's a brilliant idea. That's really brilliant!' "

When contemplating the final third of their lives, a number of my interviewees dealt on spiritual matters. I had a mean-ingful conversation with the artist Eliza-beth Murray about faith.

"As you grow older, and friends die, loss is something that you really have to come to terms with," she said. "That frightens me, I admit, and I want to have more courage with that, but I see some people's losses and I really don't know how they go on.

"I guess it's a matter of faith. I want to understand everything. Is there a God out there? I want to say there's nothing there but us, us humans, and we'd all be better off if we would accept that and then get down to business to make this better for each other. I do want to understand. Nothing makes me feel better than to feel a little flash of 'oh.' "

Elizabeth and I did not resolve this ques-tion. But we did agree that we humans have a driving force within us — a spark.

Health, work, love, passion, spirituality — these seem to be the marked characteristics of the fabulous group that I interviewed in order to cull their wisdom for this book. Oh, and of course let's not forget an excellent sense of humor. My interviewees maintained a healthy dose of humor on every topic we discussed — even mistakes.

Historian Arthur Schlesinger warmed to the subject. "My mistakes? As Omar Khayyám said in *The Rubáiyát*, 'The moving finger writes and having writ moves on. Not all your piety or wit can call back to retrace at the line, nor all your tears flush out a word of it.' In other words, if it's happened, it's happened. And I don't give a damn. It's great fun to review one's misjudgments, miscalculations, embarrassments, and mistakes."

Architect Philip Johnson took another tack. "Everybody's their own kind of damn fool. I'm full of regret, piles and piles of them, but I don't let that bother me at all. What's the point? Don't look back. Look forward. Be active, not ruminative. Find what you love and do it. That's what keeps me going."

Jane Thompson doesn't want to look back or even too far ahead. "Someone once told me that the secret of happiness is a poor memory and no foresight. That's the way I've lived all my life. If I could look ahead and see what was coming, I'd never go on. As for my past mistakes, I made them, noted them, and forgot about them. I try to ignore the downside of life. That works for me."

The lovely and effervescent Kitty Carlisle seems to have the best possible take on past mistakes and regrets. "Every morning when I'm dressed and made up and coiffed, I look in my mirror, smile and say, 'Kitty, I forgive you!' "

What a group! I am humbled by the wit and wisdom that these extraordinary people have brought to their own lives as well as to mine and to the many others that they have touched. We can all benefit and learn from their example. Note their similarities — curiosity, productivity, mental and physical fitness, a positive attitude, flexibility, a zest for life and fun, close personal relationships, spirituality, and always, a sense of humor.

When all is said and done, I'll leave the last word to Philip Johnson. When I asked if he was troubled by the onslaught of the years, he replied with sparkling eyes, "Nonsense! I never think of my age at all. There is no such thing as old age; you can quote me. I'm no different than I was fifty years ago. I'm just having more fun, which is the criterion by which I now judge all life's activities. Fun or no fun? I'm in my second childhood. I have a new freedom and independence, the two things that every person most wants. Life is teeming with possibility; you have to grab it every day."

Appendix A:

Biographies of Interviewees

MATTHEW BARRETT

Matthew Barrett, 57, the charismatic chief executive officer of Barclays Plc, was born in County Meath, Ireland, the son of a dance bandleader. After receiving his education at a Christian Brothers' School, he journeyed across the Irish Sea to London, where he was hired as a lowly clerk at the Bank of Montreal's Waterloo Place branch. His legendary rise to chairman and chief executive officer of the Bank of Montreal has cemented his reputation as a high-profile visionary and celebrity banker.

Recently separated from his second wife, he has four grown children.

J. CARTER BROWN

J. Carter Brown, director emeritus of the National Gallery of Art and chairman of the United States Commission of Fine Arts, has spent a lifetime establishing himself as the American culture czar. He served as director of the National Gallery of Art from 1969 until 1992. He is the chairman and founding member of The Pritzker Architecture Prize and the chairman and cofounder of Ovation — The Arts Network.

Brown is a trustee and member of many arts and academic institutions including the American Academy in Rome, the John F. Kennedy Center for the Performing Arts, the National Geographic Society, and the World Monuments Fund. He is the recipient of fifteen honorary degrees.

MILES AND LILLIAN CAHN

Miles Cahn, 80, and his wife Lillian, 78, founded Coach Leatherware in 1941. For thirty-nine years the Cahns designed, produced, and marketed high-quality leather items that became both a status symbol and an example of American taste and quality.

After selling Coach, the couple turned

their attention to fine cheese-making at Coach Farm in rural Pine Plains, New York. Coach Farm has become a highly regarded producer of gourmet goat cheeses.

The Cahns split their time between the farm and their New York City home, where they are avid fans of classical music and theater arts. They have three grown children and five grandchildren.

JIMMY CARTER

James Earl Carter Jr., 77, the thirty-ninth president of the United States, was born on October 1, 1924, in Plains, Georgia. His father was a farmer and businessman, his mother a registered nurse. In 1946 he graduated from the Naval Academy at Annapolis and also married his sweetheart, Rosalynn Smith.

His naval commission was followed by successful business ventures that segued into a political career that was capped by his election to the presidency in 1976.

In his postpresidential life, Jimmy Carter has authored fifteen books and has emerged as a preeminent international human rights activist and international mediator.

The Carters have four grown children and eight grandchildren.

WALTER CRONKITE

Walter Leland Cronkite Jr., 85, was born in St. Joseph, Missouri, on November 4, 1916, and raised in Houston, Texas. One of the most influential broadcasters in the history of television, Cronkite worked as a reporter and war correspondent before joining CBS News in 1950. He was managing editor and anchorman of *The CBS Evening News with Walter Cronkite* from 1962 until his retirement in 1981.

Since then he has worked as an author, speaker, narrator, host, and producer of film projects. His autobiography, *A Reporter's Life*, was printed in 1996.

DAVID CULVER

David Culver, 77, worked for four decades at the Montreal-based Alcan Aluminum Corporation, most notably as chairman and chief executive officer. Upon retirement at age 65, he created Culver and Coe, an independent investment bank, which he has nurtured successfully for the past twelve years. He is now preparing for his next career, which he claims will be either as a professional golf caddy or as a cocktail lounge piano player.

BOB DALY

Bob Daly, 63, is the chairman and chief executive officer of the Los Angeles Dodgers major league baseball team. He took over day-to-day operations in October 1999 after stepping down as chairman and chief executive officer of Warner Brothers/Warner Music.

With partner Terry Semel, Mr. Daly was one of the most powerful and successful men in the film and entertainment business for two decades. He is the recipient of many honors and awards, including the Academy Award.

He is married to composer Carole Bayer Sager.

MARY MAPLES DUNN

Mary Maples Dunn, feminist historian and noted William Penn scholar, has been a leader in women's higher education for over thirty years. Most recently, she served as the acting dean of the Radcliffe Institute for Advanced Study at Harvard University. Prior to this, she directed the Arthur and Elizabeth Schlesinger library at Radcliffe College. From 1985 until 1995 she was the president of Smith College.

Ms. Dunn is the author of a number of

books, including *Women of America: A Teacher's Guide*, *The Founding of Pennsylvania*, and *The World of William Penn*.

She is married to historian Richard S. Dunn.

BERT FIELDS

Entertainment lawyer Bert Fields, 74, is almost as famous as his celebrity clients. He has represented Hollywood megastars like John Travolta, Tom Cruise, Dustin Hoffman, and many others. He is known for his astute legal mind and flamboyant style.

Mr. Fields is also the author of two novels and a historical study of England's King Richard III and the intrigues of his court. He is currently working on a historical study of William Shakespeare as well as maintaining his show biz law practice.

He is married to Barbara and has one grown son.

HOBART GARDINER

Hobart Gardiner is the president and chief executive officer of International Executive Service Corps, a volunteer organization that pairs professionals with businesses, nonprofits, and governments in 120 developing countries.

The IESC has been called "the business-person's Peace Corps." It is the largest, most experienced, and most effective not-for-profit volunteer business development organization in the world.

IESC programs have created one million jobs worldwide.

KATHARINE GRAHAM

Born Katharine Meyer on June 16, 1917, in New York City, Katharine Graham will be remembered as one of the most important newspaper people of the twentieth century.

Daughter of financier Eugene Meyer, who purchased *The Washington Post* in 1933, she worked at the newspaper as a reporter before marrying Philip Graham in 1940. He became publisher in 1946, and Ms. Graham devoted herself to her home, husband, and four children until Philip Graham's suicide in 1963. At that time she became president of The Washington Post Company, determined to save the family business for her children. She rose to the challenge of running *The Post* in spite of criticism from skeptics who underestimated her determination to succeed. Under her stewardship, *The Washington Post* joined the hierarchy of American newspapers.

Ms. Graham won the Pulitzer Prize in 1998 for her memoir *Personal History.* She died in 2001.

DR. VICTOR GRANN

Dr. Victor Grann, 70, is the director of health outcomes research at Columbia Presbyterian's Herbert Irving Comprehensive Cancer Center. An early practitioner of clinical medical oncology, Dr. Grann became one of the world's preeminent oncologists.

In 1995, he left practice and returned to Columbia University as the first student to matriculate the health outcome track at the School of Public Health. In 1997 he was appointed to his current post at Columbia's Comprehensive Cancer Center. He also teaches at Columbia.

Dr. Grann is married to former Penguin Putnam president and chief executive officer Phyllis Grann. The couple has grown children and grandchildren.

VARTAN GREGORIAN

Vartan Gregorian, 66, an academic activist, is the current head of the Carnegie Corporation of New York, a grant-making foundation aimed at developing education, international peace, and international development. The charismatic champion of education raised The New York Public Library from fiscal ruin as president and chief executive officer from 1981 until 1989. He also led Brown University for nearly nine years.

The Iranian-born Mr. Gregorian is a winner of the National Humanities Medal. He and his wife, the former Clare Russell, have three children.

KITTY CARLISLE HART

Born Kitty Conn in New Orleans on September 3, 1915, Kitty Carlisle Hart first came to the public's attention as a singer and actress. Her career ranged from Broadway to the Marx Brothers, from the movies to the television game show *To Tell the Truth*. She also served for twenty years as New York State Council on the Arts chairwoman. Ms. Hart has long been known as a strong advocate of women's rights. She is the author of *Kitty: An Auto-*

biography and is the recipient of the National Medal of the Arts.

She continues to perform as a singer and a lecturer in a one-woman show, *Kitty Carlisle Hart — A Broadway Memory.*

Ms. Hart is the widow of Pulitzer Prize–winning playwright and director Moss Hart and is the mother of two grown children.

ELEANOR HOLTZMAN

Eleanor Holtzman, the former president and chief executive officer of the National Executive Service Corps, currently consults with cultural and arts organizations for the NESC.

Born in Brooklyn on May 7, 1931, Ms. Holtzman spent thirty-nine years in the business world, mainly in advertising agencies as a specialist in marketing and strategic planning. In 1992 she retired to the NESC, a nonprofit management consulting organization serving the nonprofit community.

She is a member of the board of directors of Americans for the Arts, chair of Elders Share the Arts, and a member of the board of the National Executive Service Corps.

She is married to Alexander Holtzman, an attorney, and has a son, Jon Holtzman.

FREDERICK (FRITZ) JACOBI

After serving as a captain in the U.S. Army Air Force air combat intelligence division during World War Two, Fritz Jacobi returned home to make a significant contribution to the national culture. He was in on the ground floor of public television, directing public-relations efforts for National Educational Television, the organization that later became the Public Broadcasting System. Jacobi's career in public relations, spanning more than forty years, also included stints as director of public relations for The National Museum of Broadcasting and director of public affairs for Columbia Business School. Since his retirement from Columbia, Jacobi has continued to work as a freelance consultant. His newest passion is tutoring New York City high school students in reading and writing.

PHILIP JOHNSON

Philip Cortelyou Johnson, one of the most influential architects of the twentieth century, was born on July 8, 1906, in Cleveland, Ohio.

As director of architecture and design for The Museum of Modern Art from 1932 until 1954, he helped establish modernism in this country and coined the term *International Style.*

Some of his most famous designs include New York City's AT&T Building, Houston's Pennzoil Place, his famous glass house in New Canaan, Connecticut, and the Seagram Building, named "building of the millennium" by *The New York Times.*

DR. NEAL KASSELL

Dr. Neal Kassell, 56, is a professor and vice chairman of neurological surgery at the University of Virginia Health Science Center. He founded the Virginia Neurological Institute in November 1993 in order to provide the best possible care at the lowest possible cost to the largest number of patients.

Dr. Kassell is a highly regarded stroke "expert" whose surgical specialties include vascular neurosurgery and benign brain tumors. Dr. Kassell and his wife, Lynn, have five children.

DAVID KEARNS

Xerox Corporation chairman until 1990, David T. Kearns, 71, is the chairman emeritus of the New American Schools. He is a well-known education activist who served as deputy secretary of education to President George Bush, on President Reagan's task force on productivity, and through long involvement with the National Urban League, Junior Achievement, and the Business Roundtable's Education Task Force. He is the coauthor, with James Harvey, of *A Legacy of Learning*, a provocative analysis of the American education system.

With his wife, Shirley, he has been active in the mentoring program. A battle with sinus cancer in the 1990's left Mr. Kearns nearly blind, with considerable hearing loss. His cancer is in remission and he claims, "I am still going strong."

C. EVERETT KOOP

Dr. C. Everett Koop, former surgeon general of the United States from 1981 until 1989, was born in Brooklyn, New York, on October 14, 1916. After earning his M.D. from Cornell University in 1941, he spent thirty-five years at Children's

Hospital in Philadelphia, where he was appointed pediatric surgeon-in-chief.

As surgeon general, he emphasized issues of smoking and health, diet and nutrition, environmental health hazards, and the importance of immunization and disease prevention.

In 1992 he founded the Koop Institute at Dartmouth University, and he continues to be a force for public health and health education.

Dr. Koop is the recipient of numerous honors and awards, including thirty-five honorary doctorates. He is the author of more than two hundred articles and books.

His family includes his wife, Elizabeth, three children, and grandchildren.

ROBERT LAYTON

Robert (Bob) Layton is the director of the Senior Lawyers Committee of the New York State Bar Association, was born in New York City in 1931. After graduating from the Yale University School of Law, Layton spent thirty-five years as a civil litigator, specializing in large, complex federal and state cases. He also represented large U.S. firms in International Chamber of

Commerce arbitrations, and has written extensively on international arbitration. During the Vietnam War, Layton won a case for the New York Civil Liberties Union, overturning General Lewis B. Hershey's selective reclassification of college student draft protesters. As director of the Senior Lawyers Committee of the ABA, Layton enables retired lawyers to become mentors for high school students.

ELIZABETH MURRAY

World-renowned American abstract artist Elizabeth Murray was born in Bloomington, Illinois, in 1940.

Her large, colorful, "shaped" paintings utilize form and relief, and exude a powerful sense of "womanly" experience and American life. Murray's first major exposure was the inclusion of her painting "Red Dakota" in the 1972 Whitney Biennial. She later traded that work for dental services. She has since been exhibited in museums and galleries around the world, including a major survey of her work in 1988 at the Whitney Museum of American Art in New York City.

Murray is heralded for her exuberant work and her idiosyncratic mind. She and her husband, poet Bob Holman, have two daughters, and Murray has a son, Dakota, from a previous marriage.

ARTHUR SCHLESINGER

Arthur Meier Schlesinger Jr., United States historian and author, was born October 15, 1917, in Columbus, Ohio.

Schlesinger, the author of sixteen books, won the Pulitzer Prize in 1945 for *The Age of Jackson* and again in 1966 for *A Thousand Days*. He is the cofounder of Americans for Democratic Action and served as presidential special assistant and speechwriter for John Fitzgerald Kennedy. At present, Schlesinger is working on his memoirs and the fourth volume of a study of the Roosevelt administration.

He resides with his wife, Alexandra, in New York City.

BEVERLY SILLS

Born Belle Miriam Silverman on May 25, 1929, in Brooklyn, New York, America's "Queen of Opera," Beverly Sills became one of America's most recognized and beloved advocates of the performing arts.

She enjoyed a childhood career as a

radio singer, then went on tour at fifteen as an opera singer. Ms. Sills joined the New York City Opera in 1955, and continued performing around the world until her retirement from the stage in 1980.

In 1979, she became the director of the New York City Opera; she was elected chairwoman of Lincoln Center for the Performing Arts in 1994. In addition to her arts endeavors, Ms. Sills has worked tirelessly for decades for the March of Dimes and other charities aimed at eliminating birth defects in children. She is married to Peter Greenough and is the mother of two and stepmother to Greenough's children from a previous marriage.

A. I. C. SMITH

Alexander (Ian) Smith, 67, is the former chairman and chief executive officer of the insurance brokerage firm Marsh & McLennan. He serves as chairman of the Central Park Conservancy.

JANE THOMPSON

Founder in 1993 of the Thompson Design Group in Boston, Jane Thompson, 74, has been a successful architect, city planner, and witness to American architectural history for almost five decades.

Her career began in the secretarial pool of The Museum of Modern Art, where she worked in the architecture department. There she encountered luminaries like Philip Johnson, I. M. Pei, Frank Lloyd Wright, and Ludwig Mies van der Rohe. Later she and her husband Ben Thompson became pivotal figures in city planning, design, and conservation. They were among the first to view architecture, design, furnishings, and food as parts of an integrated design problem.

Following her husband's stroke, Ms. Thompson continues to work as the head of her own firm. She and her husband have children, stepchildren, and grandchildren.

MIKE WALLACE

Born Myron Leon Wallace on May 9, 1918, in Brookline, Massachusetts, Mike Wallace has been the coeditor of CBS's top rated news program *60 Minutes* since its premiere on September 24, 1968.

Mr. Wallace's no-holds-barred interviewing technique has earned him a reputation as one of America's toughest investigative reporters. His list of interviewees reads like a who's who of international newsmakers.

He has received nineteen Emmy Awards, three Peabody Awards, and three DuPont Awards. He has also been inducted into the Television Academy Hall of Fame.

He lives with his fourth wife, Mary Yates; he has two grown children and grandchildren.

Appendix B:

RESOURCES FOR THE THIRD ACT*

*While the author has made every effort to provide accurate telephone numbers and Internet addresses at the time of publication, neither the publisher nor the author assumes any responsibility for errors, or for changes that occur after publication.

AMERICAN ASSOCIATION OF RETIRED PERSONS (AARP)

The AARP is the nation's leading organization for people age fifty and older. It provides information, advocacy, education, and community services to members. Publications include *My Generation*, *Modern Maturity*, and *AARP Bulletin*. Membership is $10 per year. Phone: (202) 434-3219. Address: AARP, 601 E Street NW, Washington, D.C. 20049.

AARP VOLUNTEER TALENT BANK

The AARP Volunteer Talent Bank puts the skills of senior citizens to work for agencies ranging from the Red Cross to the Nature Conservancy. Phone: (202) 434-3219. Address: VTB, 601 E Street NW, Washington, DC 20049. E-mail: vtb@aarp.org

ACCESS AMERICA FOR SENIORS

Information about the whole range of government services and benefits for seniors. Maintained by the Social Security Administration. Links to all federal agencies in all fifty states.

ALLIANCE FOR RETIRED AMERICANS

National organization created to protect the health and economic security of seniors. Membership comprises participating unions affiliated with the AFL–CIO and members of the former National Council of Senior Citizens. Other retired Americans are invited to join for a fee of $10 per year. Phone: (202) 637-5000. Address: 815 16th Street NW, Washington, D.C. 20006.

GRAY PANTHERS

Intergenerational advocacy organization dedicated to social change. Founded in

1970 by Maggie Kuhn. Phone: (800) 280-5362. Address: 733 15th Street NW, Suite 437, Washington, D.C. 20005.

HABITAT FOR HUMANITY INTERNATIONAL
HFHI is a nonprofit, ecumenical Christian housing ministry that welcomes volunteers of all faiths who are committed to Habitat's goal of eliminating poverty housing. Phone: (229) 924-6935, ext. 2551 or 2552. Address: Partner Service Center, HFHI, 121 Habitat Street, Americus, GA 31709. E-mail: publicinfo@hfhi.org

INTERNATIONAL EXECUTIVE SERVICE CORPS
The IESC pairs professionals with businesses, nonprofits, and governments in some 120 countries. Phone: (800) 243-4372. Address: IESC, P.O. Box 10005, Stamford, CT 06904.

NATIONAL EXECUTIVE SERVICE CORPS
NESC sets up consultancies tailored to the specific needs of the small to medium business and the skills of senior-level business executive volunteers. Phone: (212)

269-1234, ext. 104. Address: NESC, 120 Wall Street, New York, NY 10005.

NEW DIRECTIONS

New Directions guides senior executives and professionals into new full-time and part-time opportunities, business ventures, board directorships, consulting, humanitarian pursuits, and active retirement. Phone: (617) 523-7775. Fax: (617) 523-8197. Address: 66 Long Wharf, Boston, MA 02110-3620. E-mail: info@newdirections.com

PEACE CORPS

The Peace Corps fights hunger, disease, and lack of opportunity around the globe. The organization welcomes older applicants and values their experience, maturity, and demonstrated abilities. Brochure available online or from Peace Corps Headquarters. Phone: (800) 424-8580. Address: 1111 20th Street NW, Washington, D.C. 20526.

RETIRED AND SENIOR VOLUNTEER PROGRAM

RSVP matches people age fifty-five and older with local groups in need. Phone: (800) 424-8867. Address: RSVP, 1201 New York Avenue NW, Washington, D.C. 20525.

SERVICE CORPS OF RETIRED EXECUTIVES

SCORE enables retired business owners and executives to share their real-world knowledge with aspiring entrepreneurs. Phone: (800) 634-0245. Address: SCORE, 409 3rd Street SW, Washington, D.C. 20024.

SENIOR JOB BANK

The Senior Job Bank (Job Links for Senior Citizens) offers government and nonprofit sites for seniors.

SPRY FOUNDATION

The SPRY Foundation (Setting Priorities for Retirement Years) is a national nonprofit foundation whose mission is to help adults plan for a healthy and financially secure future. SPRY maintains the

Retirement Living Forum, an online source of aging-related information. Some publications are available. Phone: (202) 216-0401. Address: 10 G Street NE, Suite 600, Washington, DC 20002.

TECH CORPS

Tech Corps links technical experts with schools for the purpose of training the workforce of the future. Phone: (781) 687-1100. Address: Tech Corps, P.O. Box 832, Sudbury, MA 01776.

The employees of Thorndike Press hope you have enjoyed this Large Print book. All our Thorndike and Wheeler Large Print titles are designed for easy reading, and all our books are made to last. Other Thorndike Press Large Print books are available at your library, through selected bookstores, or directly from us.

For information about titles, please call:

(800) 223-1244

or visit our Web site at:

www.gale.com/thorndike
www.gale.com/wheeler

To share your comments, please write:

Publisher
Thorndike Press
295 Kennedy Memorial Drive
Waterville, ME   04901